Let's Have a Party!

EDITED BY **LAURA SCOTT** AND **BILL STEPHANI**

It's A New Year

Let's Have a Party!™

Copyright © 2005 Creative Girls Club, DRG Publishing, Berne, Indiana 46711

EXECUTIVE EDITOR Laura Scott
EDITOR Bill Stephani
PUBLISHING SERVICES MANAGER Brenda Gallmeyer
ART DIRECTOR Brad Snow
ASSISTANT ART DIRECTOR Nick Pierce

TECHNICAL EDITOR Läna Schurb
EDITORIAL ASSISTANT Joanne Neuenschwander
COPY SUPERVISOR Michelle Beck
COPY EDITOR Conor Allen

PHOTOGRAPHY Scott Campbell
PHOTO STYLIST Martha Coquat

GRAPHIC ARTS SUPERVISOR Ronda Bechinski
GRAPHIC ARTIST Klaus Rothe
GRAPHIC ARTS ASSISTANTS Allison Rothe
PRODUCTION ASSISTANTS Cheryl Kempf, Marj Morgan
TECHNICAL ARTIST Liz Morgan, Chad Summers

CHIEF EXECUTIVE OFFICER John Robinson
PUBLISHING DIRECTOR David J. McKee
BOOK MARKETING DIRECTOR Craig Scott
EDITORIAL DIRECTOR Vivian Rothe

Printed in China
First Printing: 2005
Library of Congress Number: 2004113753
ISBN: 1-931171-95-5

Hi, Girls!

Do you like parties? *Let's Have a Party!* has more than 20 awesome parties for you and your friends. Each party shows you how to make an invitation, decorations and party favors. You'll also get fun ideas for games, activities and contests, plus easy recipes for party food. Your parties will be everyone's favorite. Have fun!

Soccer Girl Party
page 72

Food Fun! page 142

Contents

6 Planning Your Party

Easy steps to get started 6

11 Birthdays & Special Occasions

Candy-Corny Costume Party
page 123

Artist Party page 97

Swim Party page 75

Twinkie Centipedes page 166

Retro Party! page 16

Edible Clay! page 151

Planning Your Party

Want to have an awesome party? With a little help from Mom or Dad, and a bit of planning, your party is sure to be the best ever!

Planning Your Party

You're going to have a party! What should you do so you and your friends will have as much fun as possible? Have a plan! Begin planning your party a few weeks ahead of time. Then everything will be ready for your party.

This book will give you *lots* of ideas for your party! There are many themes from which to choose. If you want, mix them up to make your own special, one-of-a-kind party! Each party will make lots of special memories for you and your friends.

Near the end of this book are two chapters filled with ideas for food, games and activities to enjoy at any party. But why wait for a party? You can enjoy these ideas any time!

Let's Plan a Party

Follow these 10 steps to help plan and organize your party. More details about each step follow on pages 8–10.

4 to 6 weeks before the party

1 Choose the kind of party you will have and its theme.

2 Set the date and time for your party.

3 Make a guest list.

2 to 3 weeks before the party

4 Buy or make the invitations. Send them.

5 Decide on decorations. Buy supplies you need to make them.

6 Buy favors and prizes—or buy the supplies you need to make them.

7 Plan a menu. Will you serve a full meal, or simpler snacks?

8 Choose activities or games.

1 week before the party

9 Take care of any details before the party. Double-check your lists. Put your favors or goody bags together. Do whatever you can ahead of time.

After the party

10 Don't forget to clean up!

2 Date and time

Before you set the party date, check your calendar. Are there other activities that you need to work around, like sports, vacations, lessons, holidays or your parents' work schedule? Choose a time that will be best for most of your friends. Give yourself plenty of time to plan and get ready for the party.

Set a beginning and ending time for your party. A shorter party usually works better than a longer one. Set up a general schedule for each activity. Will you have time for everything?

A party usually lasts for two to three hours—except for overnight parties, of course. Let parents know when the party will be over so they will know when to pick up your guests.

1 What kind of party should you have?

Birthday parties are very popular. Any of the ideas in this book will make a great theme for your special day! You also might want to have a party at some other time, just to get together with your friends and have fun! Look through these pages and choose the ideas that you think will be the best fit for you and your friends.

Some themes are better for summer; some are better for sleepovers; some parties are better for birthdays; some are better for just a few friends instead of a big group. … You get the picture!

Make your party your own celebration creation! You can choose one craft or activity from one party and something else from another. Pick ideas and activities that you and your friends are interested in and enjoy most.

Think about these things when you are making your party plans:

• Where will you have the party?
• Will it be indoor or outdoor?
• How much room do you have?
• How much money can you spend?
• How many friends do you want to invite?
• How much time do you have to get ready?
• How much adult help will you need?

3 Guest list

Don't make your list too long! Smaller groups are easier to handle.

Keep all your party information together in one place. Check off your list as each guest lets you know if she can come (this is called "RSVP").

List the following information for each guest:
✔ *Guest's name*
✔ *Address*
✔ *Phone*
✔ *Parent's name*
✔ *RSVP*

RSVP

RSVP is an abbreviation for the French phrase "Repondez s'il vous plait," which means "Please respond." In other words, you are asking your guests to let you know if they will be coming to your party or not. You will be able to plan better if you know how many people are coming.

4 Invitations

Send out invitations at least two weeks before the party. Include the following important information:

✔ *Kind and theme of party*
✔ *Time*
✔ *Place*
✔ *Address*
✔ *Host/hostess*
✔ *Phone number*
✔ *Special information (Should guests wear a costume or bring something to the party?)*
✔ *A date by which you'd like your guests to RSVP*

This is an example of how the inside of your invitation might look. Use colorful markers to print the information by hand, or use a computer and printer, which is faster.

5 Decorations

A party is always more fun and festive when you have decorations. But decorations cost money, even if you make your own. They also take time to make and put up. Start early and shop smart. Make a list of supplies you will need so you don't make lots of trips to the store. You can also have your guests help with some of the decorating at the party as a fun activity.

6 Favors and prizes

Party favors are small gifts you give to each guest. They can be as simple as a nut cup full of sweets, or a few crafting supplies that guests will use to make a project.

If you give prizes at your party, be sure to be fair in choosing the winners. Give all of your guests a chance to win!

7 Food

You will probably have an adult help you fix the party food. Choose things that your friends like to eat. Use recipes that will be easy to make. Try out new recipes ahead of time.

You don't need to serve a full meal. Sometimes cake, ice cream and a drink are enough.

Order a cake from the bakery several weeks before the party if you are not making it yourself. Serve it toward the end of the party, since it is usually the favorite part of the party.

If you are having activities at your party, serve the food afterward. You don't want sticky fingers when you're making a project. Spills could be a disaster!

8 Activities

Make up a sample of each craft project you will be making at your party. This will let you test how hard it is to make, and how much time it will take.

As the hostess, you will want to make sure everyone has a good time at your party. Choose activities that will include all of your guests.

Play games ahead of time (especially new ones) so you can see how long they will take. Work out any problems before the party.

Don't have guests choose teams. Instead, pick names out of a hat, or line up guests and "count off." Odd numbers are on one team and even numbers on the other.

It's a good idea to have extra games in case a game finishes early. Play games that have more than one winner. Prizes are not necessary. Enjoying the game is the best reward.

If the activities are outside, have a plan for doing something else if the weather forces you inside. If you have a larger party, you may want to ask several adults to help keep it organized.

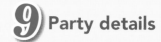

9 Party details

Start early. Begin preparing and making things for the party as soon as you can. Last-minute work will take away from your fun.

Try to find a little time each day to prepare for yor party. This is easier than doing everything the last weekend or last night before the party.

Prepare the food and finish the last-minute decorating the day before or the day of the party. Decorate the outside of the house or other party site with balloons or a sign.

Don't forget to have plenty of film for your camera. Take pictures at the beginning of the party, when everyone is freshest—especially if they are wearing costumes. Choose one person to be in charge of taking pictures because you will be too busy!

10 Cleanup

Be sure to help with the cleanup. Then your parents will be happy to say "Yes!" when you want to have another party.

Your guests will prob-ably be willing to help clean up. That will make the job fast and fun.

Birthdays and Special Occasions

Make your party awesome by using one of the cool themes in this chapter! Have fun!

Karaoke Music Party

You and your friends will all be singing stars! Sing along with your favorite songs and have a fun night being famous. Everyone gets to be a celebrity and take home a gold record.

By Reba Campbell

Invitation
  Concert Ticket
Decorations
  Music Garland
  Musical Instruments
  Gold Record
Party Favors
  Microphone
Activities
  Decorated CD Cases
Food Fun
  Diva Dogs & Dips*
  Music Munching Mix*
  Pop-Star Punch*

*Look for these recipes in the Food Fun chapter, pages 142–173. You'll find lots of EXTRA food ideas to choose from!

Invitation

Things You'll Need
* Plain white paper
* Postcards
* Black fine-tip marker
* Silver glitter spray
* Photocopier (optional)
* Glue stick
* Pencil
* Scissors

Concert Ticket

1 With pencil, trace party information pattern (page 175) on white paper and cut out. With black marker, print information, draw music symbols and fill in blanks. **Option:** *Photocopy the pattern.*

2 Glue white paper on front side of a postcard.

3 Cut notches on sides so invitation looks like a ticket.

4 Spray invitations with glitter spray.

Music Garland

1 Paint shapes. Let dry.

2 Spray shapes with clear matte sealer. Let dry.

3 Cut pink ribbon into 2-inch pieces. Bend each piece into a loop and glue ends together. Glue loop ends to the back of each wooden shape.

4 String pony beads and wooden-shapes loops on purple fuzzy yarn.

Things You'll Need
* Wooden musical shapes: quarter notes, trumpet, saxophone, guitar, treble clef, tennis racket (the number of shapes depends on how long the garland is)
* Acrylic paints: hot pink, purple and metallic silver
* Clear matte sealer
* Pink wire-edged ribbon
* Purple fuzzy yarn
* Pony beads: white and silver
* Glue
* Scissors

Musical Instruments

If you do not have musical instruments on hand, you can make these from cardboard cutouts to jazz up your party!

Using photos as a guide, draw a saxophone and guitar on cardboard. For guitar, do not draw long neck.

Things You'll Need
* Corrugated cardboard (large boxes work well)
* Hot pink spray paint
* Brass-colored spray paint
* Medium-point paint markers: white and black
* Large round jewels
* Scissors
* Glue

Saxophone

1 Paint front and back of saxophone with brass paint. Let dry.

2 See photo and draw details with black paint marker. Glue on jewels.

Guitar

1 Cut a 3 x 24-inch rectangle for neck of guitar. Glue neck to guitar.

2 Paint front and back of guitar hot pink.

3 See photo and draw lines with white paint marker. (Lines do not have to be perfectly straight.) Glue on jewels.

Decorations

Gold Record

1 Spray disc with paint. Let dry.

2 Take a photo of each guest holding a gold record. Frame photo or use it to decorate a CD case.

Things You'll Need
* 12-inch plastic foam disc, 1-inch thick
* Gold spray paint

Party Favors

Microphone

1 Gently press dowel about 1 inch into center of foam ball. Remove dowel. Put a big glob of glue into hole. Push dowel in again. Let glue dry.

2 Paint microphone. Let dry, then paint again. Let dry.

3 Pour glitter into a plastic sandwich bag. Spray ball end with sealer. While still wet, dip ball into bag to cover ball with glitter. Tap extra glitter back into bag. Let dry.

Things You'll Need
For each microphone:
* 3-inch plastic foam ball
* 6-inch piece of ⅝-inch dowel
* Paint: purple, pink, black, silver
* Matte sealer
* Glitter
* Small foam brush
* Glue
* Plastic sandwich bag

Decorated CD Cases

CD #1
Decorate front of CD case with paint markers. Cut yellow card stock to fit inside CD case. Slip into CD case.

CD #2
Cut card stock to fit inside CD case. Decorate card stock with die cut and marker. Slip into CD case.

CD #3
1 Cut musical note paper to fit inside CD case.

2 Cut photo to desired size. Glue on pink card stock. Cut around card stock, leaving a ¼-inch border.

3 Glue cardstock to music notepaper. Slip into CD case.

Things You'll Need
★ Blank CD case
★ Medium-tip paint markers: your choice of colors
★ Yellow card stock

Things You'll Need
★ Blank CD case
★ Hot pink card stock
★ Quarter note paper die cut
★ Black marker

Things You'll Need
★ Blank CD case
★ Musical note paper
★ Hot pink card stock
★ Photo
★ Glue stick

CD #3

CD #1

music party

CD #2

Food Fun! Even stars have to eat! Check out our recipes for *Diva Dogs & Dips*, *Music Munching Mix* and *Pop Star Punch* on page 142–173.

Retro Party

Retro means "to go backward," so plan a party that takes you back in time! Dress up like your favorite celebrity from the 1950s, '60s, '70s or '80s. Make fun projects and eat your favorite food that is still "groovy" today!

By Karen Booth

Invitation
  Tie-Dye Invitations
Decorations
  Smiley Faces
  Groovy Napkins & Table
    Cover
Party Favors
  Macramé Key Chain
Activities
  Tie-Dyed T-Shirt
Food Fun
  Dogs in Blankets*
  Root Beer Floats*
  Rainbow Gelatin Cubes*
  S'mores*

*Look for these recipes in the Food Fun chapter, pages 142–173. You'll find lots of EXTRA food ideas to choose from!

Far out.....Rachel's having an Outa Sight Retro Party!
Learn to Macrame-COOL-Tie Dye a T-shirt-GROOVY-watch some TV oldies and have lots of fun with friends.
Please come in a Retro Costume. (just look in Mom or Dad's closet!)
Bring a washed white cotton T-shirt and don't forget your sleeping bag this Friday at 4:30 pm.
BE THERE OR BE SQUARE!

Tie-Dye Invitations

Let's Begin

1 Cover your work table with plastic or newspapers.

2 Find the center of the paper towel. Pull edges down to make a point. Twist gently.

3 Use cord to tie tight bands around paper towel.

4 Mix water with paint in a small container until it is as thick as ink. Use a different container for each color.

5 Brush different parts of the paper towel with different colors. Let set for 1 hour.

6 Gently remove cord and unravel it. Unfold paper towel. Set it aside to dry.

7 Gently pull the layers or paper towel apart. You can use both sheets for separate invitations.

Finish Your Invitation

1 Flatten out the dyed paper towel. Spread glue stick over entire front of card. Lay paper towel on top of glue. Use scissors to trim extra paper towel from edges.

2 Use white glue to glue a felt smiley face to front of invitation.

3 Use the pens or a computer to print inside of invitation on white paper. Cut out with scissors. Glue inside invitation with glue stick.

4 Decorate envelope with retro felt stickers.

Things You'll Need
* Plastic or newspapers to cover work table
* 2-ply paper towels
* Soft cotton cord
* Acrylic craft paints—bright colors
* Paintbrushes
* Containers
* Felt smiley faces*
* Retro felt stickers*
* Cards and envelopes in bright colors
* Glue stick
* White glue
* Felt-tip pens or computer with printer
* Plain white paper
* Scissors

*CPE Stiffened Eazy-Felt Smiley Faces (#FS32) and Stick-it-Felt Retro felt stickers (#FSSIF4) were used to make this project.

Decorations

Smiley Faces

1 Lay bowl face down on foam. Trace around it several times to make circles.

2 Cut out circles. Glue two eyes to each circle.

3 Draw a smile on each circle with dimensional paint. Let dry.

4 Place tape onto back of each face. Press each face onto the wall, door or tabletop. Or, tape or glue faces to colored streamers and hang in a doorway or window.

Things You'll Need
* Yellow fun foam
* Large wiggly eyes
* White glue
* Shiny black dimensional paint
* Small bowl
* Pencil
* Scissors
* Masking tape
* Bright crepe paper streamers (optional)

Groovy Napkins & Table Cover

Peel backing from a felt sticker. Stick it on the corner of a napkin. Repeat to make as many napkins as you want.

Stick felt stickers on a paper table covering that matches your napkins. Or, tie-dye an old sheet for a funky tablecloth.

Things You'll Need
* Bright yellow paper napkins
* Paper tablecloth or old sheet
* Retro felt stickers*
*CPE Stick-it-Felt Retro felt stickers (#FSSIF4) were used to make this project.

Macramé Key Chain

1 Cut two pieces of cord, each 40 inches long.

2 Fold pieces in half. Loop them through key chain ring (see Fig. 1).

Fig. 1   **Fig. 2**

3 Keep cords tight by hooking the ring onto something, taping it down or having a friend hold the ring. The two center cords stay in the middle. You will tie with the outside cords.

Things You'll Need

For each key chain:
- Jute, hemp *or* cord
- Key chain ring
- Ruler *or* measuring tape
- Scissors
- Pony beads *or* other beads with larger holes

4 Bring the left cord over two middle cords and under right cord (Fig. 2).

5 Bring the right cord under left cord, over two middle cords, then over left cord (Fig. 3).

6 Pull ends of cords in Fig. 3 tight to form first part of knot.

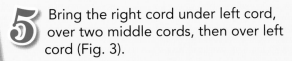

Fig. 3   **Fig. 4**

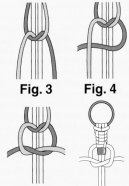

Fig. 5   **Fig. 6**

7 Follow Figs. 4 and 5 to make a complete knot. You'll reverse what you did in Figs. 2 and 3. If you knot in only one direction, the project will spiral.

8 *Add beads:* Thread bead onto two middle cords and push against knot (Fig. 6). Tie a knot, leaving a loose loop around bead. Tie a few more knots, then add a bead. Or, add another bead directly after the last.

9 When you are comfortable with basic knots, get creative with knotting the ends.

Tie-Dyed T-Shirt

Before Your Party

Ask everyone to wear old clothes, or bring an old shirt or apron to wear. Work outdoors if you can. The dye will stain the floor, clothes, furniture, etc.

Let's Begin

 1 Read all instructions that come with tie-dye kit.

 2 Fold or crumple shirt or bandana however you want. Use rubber bands to hold the folds in your project. The tighter the rubber band, the more white will show.

3 Put on gloves. Mix the soda ash liquid following the kit's instructions. Soak project in liquid.

4 Leave gloves on. Follow kit's instructions to mix dyes.

5 After soaking is finished, wring out project.

6 Cover work table with plastic. Everyone should wear gloves and old clothes.

7 Squirt dyes onto project. Make colorful patterns and designs. Look at the kit box for ideas.

8 When finished, wrap each project in a plastic bag so it will stay wet. Let set at least 4 hours. If you want really deep colors, let it set for 8 hours.

9 Follow kit instructions for rinsing project, taking off bands and washing it.

Things You'll Need

* Tie-dye kit
* Extra rubber gloves for all your guests
* White cotton T-shirt or white bandana, washed and dried without using fabric softener
* Plastic table covering
* Plastic bags

*Rainbow Rock's Ultimate Tie-Dye Kit (#RR 17782) was used to make this project.

Food Fun! Snacks that were popular in the '70s or '80s will hit the spot! Check pages 142–173 for recipes for *Dogs in Blankets, Mini Pizza Bites, Root Beer Floats, Rainbow Gelatin Cubes* and that snacking classic, *S'mores.*

Retro Party ❤ Retro Party ❤ Retro Party ❤ Retro Party ❤ Retro Party ❤ Retro Party

Slumber Fun Sleepover

Bring your sleeping bags and pillows and get ready for a night of unforgettable fun! Just remember: You should try to get *some* sleep!

By Sandy L. Rollinger

SURPRISE

BIRTHDAY SLEEP-OVER PARTY

BIRTHDAY GIRL _____
DATE _____
TIME : FROM ____ PM TO ____ AM
BRING YOUR PJ'S, SLEEPING BAG, AND PILLOW TO: _____ HOUSE

Invitation
  Sweet Slumber Cloud
Decorations
  Slumber Fun
    Centerpiece
  Slumber Fun Table
    Accents
Party Favors
  Slumber Socks
Activities
  Marshmallow Toss
Food Fun
  Star and Moon
    Cookies*
  Milk
  Hot Chocolate with
    Marshmallows
  Pretzels
  Veggie Sticks with Dip

Look for this recipe in the Food Fun chapter, pages 142–173. You'll find lots of EXTRA food ideas to choose from!

Invitation

Sweet Slumber Cloud

1 Trim edges of card so that invitation is shaped like a cloud, about 5 x 3⅛ inches. Fold should be on left edge.

2 Pour a little blue paint onto paper plate. Dab sponge into paint. Dab sponge onto folded paper towel until most of the paint comes off.

▶CONTINUED ON PAGE 22

►CONTINUED FROM PAGE 21

 Dab sponge lightly around edges on front of invitation. Set aside to dry.

4 Trace patterns for small star and moon (page 176) onto white paper. Cut out. Trace around one star on back of blue parchment and one moon on back of yellow paper. Cut out.

5 Using computer or a black felt-tip pen, print "SURPRISE" and "BIRTHDAY SLEEPOVER PARTY" on blue parchment. Cut out each phrase.

6 Using computer or pen, print out party information (see photo). Cut out.

7 Glue party information inside invitation. Glue moon, star and other phrases to front of invitation as shown.

8 Glue star spangle to paper star. Glue blue rhinestone star to moon for eye. Glue other blue star to spangle. Glue clear star to invitation near top.

9 Draw smile on moon with white paint. Add swirls and curlicues of white and glittery paint to front of invitation. Let dry.

Things You'll Need

* 4 x 5-inch white invitation card with envelope with fold along 4-inch edge
* Light blue parchment card stock
* Yellow print decorative paper
* Light blue craft paint
* Round painting sponge or small piece of sponge
* 1 clear and 2 blue small rhinestone stars
* 1½-inch silver star spangle
* Glittery dimensional paint
* Shiny white dimensional paint
* Computer with printer or black felt-tip pen
* Paper plate
* Paper towels
* Pencil
* Scissors
* Glue

Sweet Slumber Songs

Serenade your friends with a collection of sweet bedtime tunes! Burn them onto a CD before your party. It will make perfect background music!

Dream On
Dream Baby
Sleepy-Time Gal
Dream a Little Dream
Sleepless in Seattle
Lullaby of Broadway
Lullaby and Goodnight
Daydream Believer

Slumber Fun Centerpiece

Moon & Star Cookies

Note: *Ask an adult to help you with the oven and hot cookie sheet when you bake the cookies.*

1 Roll out cookie dough ¼–⅓ inch thick. Cut star and moon shapes with cookie cutters.

2 Use spatula to move cookies onto cookie sheet. Stick a lollipop stick in side of each cookie. Bake cookies following directions on package.

3 Using pot holder or oven mitt, carefully remove hot cookies from oven. Use spatula to move cookies to wire rack to cool.

4 Frost cookies with white frosting. Decorate stars with blue sugar. Decorate moon with yellow sugar.

Things You'll Need
Moon and Star Cookies:
* Refrigerated sugar cookie dough
* Star and moon cookie cutters
* Rolling pin
* White paper lollipop sticks
* Cookie sheet lined with baking parchment
* Spatula
* Oven
* Pot holders
* Wire rack
* Tub of white frosting
* Yellow and blue sugar

Cloud Ornaments

1 Write song titles or other phrases on blue parchment with felt-tip pen (or print them out on computer). Leave enough room between titles to cut out a cloud shape around each.

2 Cut out simple cloud shapes around titles. They should measure about 3½ x 1¾ inches. Check the cloud pattern (page 176) to make sure your paper clouds will fit on it with room to spare.

3 Trace cloud pattern (page 176) onto white paper. Cut it out. Trace around pattern onto white craft foam eight times. Cut out with scissors. Erase any pencil marks.

Things You'll Need
Cloud Ornaments:
* White craft foam
* Light blue parchment card stock
* Computer with printer or black felt-tip pen
* Glittery dimensional paint
* Pencil
* Scissors
* Plain white paper
* 8 white paper lollipop sticks
* Wire cutters
* Craft glue

▶ **CONTINUED ON PAGE 24**

Decorations

▶CONTINUED FROM PAGE 23

Things You'll Need

Wreath:

* ✴ 12-inch plastic foam wreath
* ✴ Adhesive dots or craft glue
* ✴ ½-inch double-sided tape
* ✴ Small blue and clear rhinestone stars
* ✴ Fluffy craft stuffing
* ✴ String of tiny clear Christmas lights
* ✴ 1½-inch silver star spangles
* ✴ 1½-inch blue gingham ribbon
* ✴ Wire nippers
* ✴ Tape measure

4 Glue a blue cloud in center of each foam cloud. Decorate clouds with swirls of glitter paint. Let dry.

5 Ask an adult to help you trim eight lollipop sticks with wire cutters. They should measure 3¾ inches. Glue one to back of each cloud.

Wreath

1 Use tape measure to measure length around wreath. Cut a piece of ribbon that long, adding about ½ inch so ends will overlap.

2 Wrap double-sided tape around wreath. Cover sides of wreath with ribbon, pressing it onto tape. Cut tiny piece of tape to hold ribbon end in place.

3 Pull handfuls of stuffing and glue them over edge of wreath. Use only a little glue. Don't mash stuffing flat. You want to make fluffy clouds.

4 Pull another fluffy lump of stuffing to rest in center of wreath.

5 Glue a star rhinestone in center of each star bangle. Glue bangles to stuffing. Glue a few clear star rhinestones to stuffing. Let dry.

6 Poke sticks of cookies and clouds through stuffing into foam wreath.

Add Starlight!

1 Before guests arrive, arrange Christmas lights on table so that they will fit in center of wreath. Set wreath over lights, leaving light plug free.

2 Plug lights into nearest outlet. They will "sparkle" through the clouds.

Safety Note: *Use an extension cord if needed. Don't put cord where you will have to walk over it. Don't cover the cord with sleeping bags, pillows or blankets. Unplug the wreath before you go to sleep.*

Slumber Fun Table Accents

Place Mat

 Trim edges of craft foam to make cloud shape.

 Pour a little blue paint onto paper plate. Dab sponge into paint. Dab sponge onto folded paper towel until most of the paint comes off.

 Dab sponge lightly around edges of place mat. Set aside to dry.

Stars & Moon

 Trace patterns for small and large stars and moon (page 176) onto white paper. Cut out. Trace around one large star and four small stars on back of blue parchment.

 Trace one moon on back of solid yellow card stock. Cut out.

 Trace another moon on back of yellow print paper. Cut out, cutting a little inside pencil lines so this moon is smaller. Glue a star spangle to each parchment star. Glue a rhinestone star to each spangle.

Outline all parchment stars with squiggly lines of glitter paint. On large star, add a squiggly outline of shiny white paint inside glittery outline. Let dry.

Glue print moon in center of solid moon. Glue on star rhinestone for eye. Outline smaller moon with squiggly line of glittery paint. Add smile with shiny white paint.

Finish Place Mat

Glue small stars and moon to place mat as shown. Add squiggles of glittery paint and white paint around edges of place mat.

Finish Napkin Ring

 Shape ribbon in a ring. Where ends overlap, tape them together with double-sided tape.

Attach another piece of tape to this seam, and press napkin ring onto place mat.

Glue large star to top of napkin ring. Roll napkin and put in ring.

Things You'll Need

For each place mat:

* 12 x 18-inch sheet white craft foam
* Light blue parchment card stock
* Solid yellow card stock
* Yellow print decorative paper
* Light blue craft paint
* Round painting sponge or small piece of sponge
* Craft glue
* ½-inch double-sided tape
* 6 blue small rhinestone stars
* 5 silver 1½-inch star spangles
* 4 inches 1½-inch-wide blue gingham ribbon
* Yellow paper dinner napkin
* Glittery dimensional paint
* Shiny white dimensional paint
* Computer with printer or black felt-tip pen
* Paper plate
* Paper towels
* Pencil
* Scissors
* Glue

Slumber Socks

Party Favors

Moon

 Trace pattern for moon (page 176) onto white paper. Cut out.

 Trace around moon on back of solid yellow card stock. Cut out. Trace another moon on back of yellow print paper. Cut out, cutting a little inside pencil lines so this moon is smaller.

 Glue print moon in center of solid moon. Glue on star rhinestone for eye. Outline smaller moon with squiggly line of glittery paint. Add smile with shiny white paint.

Socks

 Using needle and thread, sew a small bow to cuff of each sock with two or three stitches. (Remember to put them on opposite sides.)

 Sew star button over center of bow on each sock.

Put It Together!

 Cut a piece of tape to fit across one end of ribbon. Press tape into place. Form ribbon into a ring, overlapping ends and pressing tape to hold ring closed.

 Cut another piece of tape and press it over seam in ribbon ring. Press moon onto tape.

 Fold socks in half and slip them into ribbon ring as shown.

Things You'll Need

For each favor:

* 1 pair new white sport socks
* Solid yellow card stock
* Yellow print decorative paper
* Small blue rhinestone star
* 8 inches 1½-inch-wide blue gingham ribbon
* Glittery dimensional paint
* Shiny white dimensional paint
* 2 blue star buttons
* 2 small bows made from ¼-inch yellow ribbon
* Pencil
* Scissors
* Plain white paper
* Craft glue
* Double-sided tape
* Needle and white sewing thread
* Scissors

Activities

Marshmallow Toss

 Lay a line of tape on floor. Six feet from tape, set up a row of mugs, one for each guest.

 Line guests up behind tape, facing mugs. Give each guest some miniature marshmallows.

 Set timer for three minutes. See who can throw the most marshmallows into her mug. But don't step over the line!

Spa Party

Invite your friends to come over dressed in their favorite robes. All of you can then spend a few hours getting pampered! You'll be refreshed and relaxed after everyone gets a strawberry-and-banana facial mask!

By Karen Booth

Invitation

Spa Party Invitation

Things You'll Need

* Plain card with envelope
* Sea-theme paper*
* White paper
* Colored markers or computer with printer
* Glue stick
* Scissors
* Pencil
* Ruler

*ProvoCraft Sea Parties Water Scrapbooking Paper was used to make this project.

1 Place card on sea-theme paper. Trace around it twice.

2 Spread glue stick on paper and press one on front of card and one on back of card.

3 Print "SPA" letters and "Special Party Invitation" with colored markers on white paper or use a computer with printer. *Option: Add borders around letters.*

4 Cut a square or rectangle around letters or words. See photo and glue them to front of card and/or envelope.

5 Print party information with colored markers on white paper or use a computer with printer. *Option: Add borders around letters.* Cut a rectangle around information and glue to inside of card.

Special Party Announcement

...sie invites you
...n afternoon of
...pering and Projects!
...me @ Noon wearing
... favorite Robe.....
...e you Saturday!

Invitation
  Spa Party Invitation
Decorations
  Spa Table
Party Favors
  Oatmeal Face Scrub
Activities
  Layered Bath Salts
  Manicures
  Strawberry-Banana
    Mask
Food Fun
  Veggie Platter with
    Lemon Dill Dip*
  Cottage Cheese & Salsa
    Omelet*
  Fresh Fruit with Yogurt
    Cream*
  Sparkling Water with
    Frozen Strawberries*

Look for these recipes in the Food Fun chapter, pages 142–173. You'll find lots of EXTRA food ideas to choose from!

Spa Table

Set Your Table

Cover table with your favorite table covering. Arrange candles, flowers and shells down the center. Add beads, decorator marbles or bits of sea glass. Place a napkin, fork and plate of fresh fruit at each place.

Note: Always *ask an adult for help when lighting candles.*

Another Idea: Door Signs

Paint colorful signs for the wall or doors that say "Cassie's Day Spa" or "The Spa Experience." Decorate with sea-theme paper and colorful borders.

Food Fun!

Treat your guests to great food, just like the real spas do! Check pages 142–173 for recipes for *Veggie Platter with Lemon Dill Dip, Cottage Cheese & Salsa Omelette, Fresh Fruit with Yogurt Cream* and *Sparkling Water with Frozen Strawberries.*

Oatmeal Face Scrub

Stamp Bag

 1 Fold a piece of wax paper. Place it inside muslin bag to separate sides of bag while painting. Lay bag on hard, flat surface.

2 Brush shamrock and amethyst pearl paints on different sections of seashell stamp.

3 Press stamp firmly onto muslin bag. Lift stamp straight up. Let dry. Remove wax paper.

Make Facial Scrub

1 Place equal amounts of oatmeal and skim milk powder in blender. Place lid on blender.

 2 Run blender for several seconds, until oatmeal flakes are broken into small bits.

Put It All Together

 1 Pour about ⅓ cup of mixture into each small plastic bag. Place a bag inside muslin bag.

 2 For tag, cut a 1 x 3-inch piece from card stock. Punch a small circle in one end. Print "Face Scrub" on tag. **Option:** *Use letter stickers.* Insert one ribbon of pouch through hole. Tie ribbon in a bow.

 3 Make sure all of your guests have the following directions:

To use scrub: *Pour about 1 teaspoon of facial scrub into the palm of your hand. Add a few drops of water to make a paste. Dip your fingertips into the mixture and gently scrub your face. Rinse well with clear water.*

Things You'll Need

For each packet:
* Oatmeal flakes
* Skim milk powder
* Small self-sealing plastic bag
* Plain small muslin bag
* White card stock
* Small circle punch
* Alphabet stickers (optional)
* Seashell rubber stamp*
* Fabric pearl paint*: shamrock and amethyst
* Small paintbrushes
* Wax paper
* Blender

*A seashell Chunky Stamp and Tulip Fabric Paints from Duncan Enterprises were used to make this project.

Things You'll Need

* Glass jars with lids or corks
* Epsom salts
* Sea salt
* Liquid food coloring
* Essential oils (optional)
* Glass or metal mixing bowls
* Spoons
* Raffia
* Seashore rub-on transfers (optional)*
* Shrinking plastic
* Starfish and seahorse rubber stamps*
* Fabric pearl paints*: lemon zest, carnation pink, shamrock, amethyst
* Small paintbrushes
* Black fine-tip marker
* Small circle punch
* Craft stick
* Scissors
* Baking sheet lined with foil
* Oven
* Pot holders
* Cooling rack

*Chunky Stamps and Tulip Seashore Rub-On Transfers and Fabric Paints from Duncan Enterprises were used for this project.

Layered Bath Salts

Mix the Bath Salts

1   Measure equal amounts of Epsom salts and sea salt into bowls. Use a separate bowl for each color. Mix well.

2   Add several drops of food coloring to each bowl. Stir well. Add a few drops of essential oil to the salts if you wish. Mix well.

Decorate the Jar

1   Clean glass jar and lid very well.

2   Cut out pictures from sheet of rub-ons. Leave a border of at least ⅛ inch around each picture.

3   Peel off backing sheet from rub-on. Lay rub-on on jar. Press it in place with your fingers. Rub edge of craft stick over entire picture.

4   Slowly lift off clear film. If parts of design do not stick, press back onto jar and rub with craft stick again.

Make the Tags

1   Brush shamrock and amethyst pearl paints onto separate sections of the seahorse stamp.

2   Stamp several seahorses on shrinking plastic so you can choose the best. Let dry.

3   Brush lemon zest and carnation pink pearl paints onto separate sections of starfish stamp.

4   Repeat step 2 using starfish stamp.

5   Draw around outline of seahorses and starfish with black marker. Using marker, print "Bath Salts" across middle of seahorse. Let dry.

6   Cut out starfish and seahorses with scissors. Using circle punch, make a hole at the top of each piece, near the edge. Place pieces on baking sheet lined with foil.

7   *Note:* Ask an adult to help when using the oven. Preheat oven to 275 degrees. Bake pieces in oven 3–5 minutes to make them shrink.

Using pot holders, remove cookie sheet. Set it on a cooling rack.

 When pieces have cooled, choose the best ones to use on jars.

Put It All Together

 Use spoon to put salts in jars. Add layers of different colors until the jar is full. Put on lid or insert cork.

 Thread several strands of raffia through hole in tag. Wrap raffia around the neck of the jar and tie it in a bow.

Make sure all of your guests have the following directions:
To use bath salts: Sprinkle about 2 tablespoons of salts over bath water. Stir water to dissolve.

Another Idea:
Manicures or Pedicures

Collect small bottles of nail polish, cotton balls, emery boards, nail buffers and nail polish remover in small baskets. Give each other manicures or pedicures. How about trying some fun fingernail decals?

Things You'll Need
* Strawberries
* Bananas
* Small bowl and fork for each guest
* Towel for each guest
* Paper tissue

Strawberry-Banana Mask

 Crush three slices of strawberry and two slices of banana in a bowl with fork.

 Have each guest wrap a towel around her shoulders. Spread the mask on each other's faces or let girls do it themselves.

 Let mask sit for two minutes. Wipe most of mask off with a paper tissue. Rinse the rest off with cool water.

Girlfriends Party

Girlfriends are forever! You'll always remember the fun time you had at this Girlfriends Party when you make charm bracelets and deco books together.

By Jill DeAnn Evans

Invitation
"GirlFriend, Please come ..."
Decorations
Make It Fun & Funky!
Party Favors
Girlfriend Deco Books
Activities
Girlfriend Charm Bracelets
Slippers or PJs Contest
"Good Gossip"
"You Go, Girlfriend"
Food Fun
Chicken Salad Sandwiches*
Crisp, Cold Veggie Tray*
Chips and Dip
Strawberry Lemonade
Girlfriend Cupcakes*

Look for these recipes in the Food Fun chapter, pages 142–173. You'll find lots of EXTRA food ideas to choose from!

Invitation

"GirlFriend, Please come ..."

Let's Begin!

Fold the neon green card stock in half so that it makes a card 5½ x 4¼ inches. The fold should be on the left edge.

Cover

1 Use your computer and printer to print "GirlFriend, Please come ..." on plain paper as shown. (Or you can use gel pens or markers.) Cut out with scissors so that words are in

Things You'll Need
For each invitation:
* ½ sheet (4¼ x 11 inches) neon green card stock
* Plain white paper
* Charms patterns (page 177)
* Glue pen
* Mini "pinking shears" paper edgers
* Extra-fine pink neon glitter
* 12 inches light green metallic ⅛-inch ribbon or cord
* Computer with color printer (optional)
* Gel pens or fine-tip markers: black, plus assorted neon colors
* Scissors
* Ruler
* Pencil
* Photocopier (optional)

GirlFriend,
Please come…

Join the GIRLS for a
Fabulous
Slumber Party of Friendship

555 East Saratoga Road
Address

Friday, September 22nd at 6:00 pm
through
Saturday, September 23rd at 10:00 am
Time

Girlfriend at 555-5555 by September 15th
Please **RSVP**

Make It Fun & Funky!

Cut large hearts, smiley faces, telephones and groovy swirls from posterboard, card stock or paper. See the patterns on page 177 for ideas. You can enlarge those designs on a photocopier if you want.

Color them in bright colors. Hang them all over with poster putty. Or hang them from streamers hanging from the ceiling or doorway.

center of a 5½ x 3-inch rectangle. Trim long edges with "pinking shears" paper edgers.

2 Photocopy charm patterns (page 177). Color one of the charms in fun neon colors. Cut it out with scissors.

3 Glue the paper strip and charm to front of invitation using the glue pen.

4 Lay a clean piece of paper on your work table. Lay invitation on the paper. Draw around the charm with the glue pen. Sprinkle glitter over the glue. Turn invitation over and tap it so that extra glitter falls on the paper. Bend the paper into a funnel and pour the glitter back into its container.

5 Working as you did in step 4, draw a wavy line across the white paper with your glue pen. Cover it with pink glitter.

Inside

1 Use your computer and printer (or gel pens or markers) to print party information on plain white paper:

Join the GIRLS for a

Fabulous

Slumber Party of Friendship

2 Below this, print your address, the date and time of your party, and a phone number and deadline for RSVPs.

3 Print the information in an area no bigger than 3½ x 3¼ inches.

4 Cut out with scissors so that words are in center of a 4½ x 3½-inch rectangle. Trim short edges with paper edgers.

5 Glue the paper inside the invitation using the glue pen.

Finishing

Tie the metallic green ribbon around the center of the card, at the fold. Tie the ends in a bow on the front.

Girlfriend Deco Books

Before Your Party

Make a book for each party guest. Each book should have at least one page for each guest. If you're having 10 guests, each book should have at least 10 pages, not counting the covers.

Let's Begin

1 Cut card stock in half down its length. Pieces should measure 4¼ x 11 inches.

2 Fold each piece in half and run your finger along the crease. The folded pieces will measure 4¼ x 5½ inches.

3 Open folded pages up. Using a pencil and ruler, mark two dots right on the crease. One should be ¾ inch from the left edge. The other should be ¾ inch from the right edge. Use the paper punch to punch a hole at each dot.

4 Repeat step 3 on all pieces of card stock.

5 Stack as many pages as you need for a book. The holes should line up.

6 Cut a 12- to 15-inch piece of cord. Thread one end through one set of holes, from the inside of the book to the outside. Thread the other end of cord through the other set of holes.

7 Knot the cord ends together outside the book, or tie them in a bow. Thread a pony bead onto the ends of the cord if you want.

Things You'll Need

To make the books:
* Bright neon card stock in colors of your choice (we used purple, pink, blue, green, yellow and orange)
* ⅛-inch circle paper punch
* Brightly colored rat-tail craft cord
* Brightly colored pony beads
* Glue
* Scissors

To decorate the pages:
* Assorted small stickers, including alphabet stickers
* Assorted small paper die cuts
* Scraps of fabric and decorative paper
* Colored pens, glitter pens, markers
* Glitter, sequins
* Charms
* Colorful craft wire, ribbon
* Small buttons
* Glue, double-sided tape
* Scissors

At Your Party

Set out all your supplies—glue, scissors, stickers, pens, ribbon and other things. Give a book to each guest. Then, pass around your books and have each girlfriend decorate a page or two in each book.

Girlfriend Charm Bracelets

Before Your Party

 1 Use a photocopier to make a copy of the charms patterns (page 177) for each guest.

 2 Attach a lobster claw clasp to one end of each bracelet using the needle-nose pliers.

 3 Ask an adult for help if you need it.

 4 Read all the instructions for coloring and baking the shrinking plastic.

Ask an adult to be on hand to help with moving the charms in and out of the oven, and to help attach the rings with pliers.

Let's Begin!

 1 Lay shrinking plastic over pattern page on work table. Rough, dull side of shrinking plastic should face up.

 2 Trace and color patterns. Or, sketch your own original designs. Add lettering with a fine-tip permanent marker or dark-colored pencil.

 3 Cut out plastic charms with scissors. Round off any points or sharp corners.

 4 Use the small circle punch to punch a hole near the edge of each charm.

 5 Following the instructions that came with the shrinking plastic, bake the charms: Preheat the oven, and put the charms on the foil-lined cookie sheet. Use pot holders when moving the pan, or ask an adult to help.

 6 Use pot holders to remove the cookie sheet from the oven (or ask an adult to do that for you). Set the sheet on a cooling rack. Let the charms cool.

7 Use the pliers to attach a split ring to each charm. Then attach each split ring to the bracelet.

Things You'll Need

For each charm bracelet:
* 1 sheet shrinking plastic
* Charms patterns
* Good-quality colored pencils in bright neon colors (See Note below.)
* Fine-tip permanent marker
* Small scissors
* ⅛-inch circle hole punch
* Regular circle hole punch
* About 7 inches of silver jack chain (See Note below.)
* 6mm silver split rings
* 13mm lobster claw clasp
* Needle-nose pliers or jewelry pliers
* Cookie sheet covered with foil
* Pot holders
* Cooling rack
* Oven

Note: Don't use cheap, waxy colored pencils or wax- or oil-based coloring products. They can catch fire in the oven. Silver jack chain is inexpensive. You can find it at home improvement stores.

Slippers or PJs Contest

Have a "beauty contest" for pajamas or slippers! Give prizes for "silliest," "most like the wearer," "furriest," "warmest," "most elegant," etc.

If you choose to have this contest, be sure to put a reminder on the invitation to bring PJs and slippers.

"Good Gossip"

"If you can't say something nice, then don't say anything at all!" Make all your girlfriends feel good by sharing something nice about them.

Have the *first* girl in line whisper something sweet, kind and/or positive about the *last* girl in line to the *second* girl in line. Pass along the sweet gossip to each girl until it reaches the *next to last* girl in line. She will repeat the sweet gossip so everyone can hear.

Now—how much is it the same, or how much has it changed from the original compliment?

At this point, the *last* girl moves to the other end of the line and becomes the *first* girl, and the game is repeated. Continue until all the girls have heard some sweet "good gossip" about themselves.

"You Go, Girlfriend"

Keep this one a secret until your party is almost over! Near the end of your party, ask each guest to write down on a piece of paper the name of a girl they thought showed the most kindness, was most helpful and gracious during the entire party. Tally the names and present the winner with a small prize.

LISA ★ YOU ARE KIND TO EVERYONE IN OUR CLASS!

Food Fun! Your guests will love *Chicken Salad Sandwiches* and *Girlfriend Cupcakes*. See pages 142–173 for recipes and yummy ideas.

Sweet Shoppe

This party is sweet, really sweet! You'll make a cookie pizza and decorate it for the yummiest party ever!

By Lorine Mason

Invitation

Cookie Pouch

1 To make the pouch, lay beige card stock on worktable so that longer edges are at top and bottom.

2 Lay ruler across card stock, near top. With pencil, mark a small dot at 1 inch, 6½ inches, and 7½ inches from left edge.

3 Mark the same dots along bottom edge of card stock.

4 To "score" lines, place ruler along dots 1 inch from edge. Press letter opener or stylus along ruler to score card stock from top to bottom.

5 Repeat step 4 to "score" lines on card stock 6½ inches and 7½ inches from edge.

6 Glue strip of cookie-print paper to card stock, covering line at 1-inch mark.

▶ CONTINUED ON PAGE 40

Things You'll Need

* 5 x 12-inch beige card stock
* 4 x 5-inch ivory card stock
* 2 x 5-inch strip cookie dough print paper
* 3½ x 5-inch strip red candy-stripe print paper
* Black felt-tip marker or computer with printer
* Clear cellophane bag
* Miniature chocolate chip cookies
* Letter opener or stylus
* Decorative-edge scissors: wavy
* Scissors
* Glue stick
* Pencil
* Ruler
* Stapler

Invitation
  Cookie Pouch
Decorations
  Cups & Place Mats
  Napkin Rings
  Place Cards
Party Favor
  Cookie Bouquet
Activities
  Cookie Pizza
Food Fun
  Cookie Pizza
  Marbleized Milk*

*Look for this recipe in the Food Fun chapter, page 171. You'll find lots of EXTRA food ideas to choose from!

Kimbrely's Sweet Shoppe
Birthday Party
August 19th, 2:00 - 4:00
204 Sunny Drive
Welcome, Va.
(703) 222-2222

Cups & Place Mats

1 For cookies, use circle punch to make 12 circles from cookie paper.

2 For place mat, cut out a 12-inch circle from white card stock with corkscrew scissors.

3 Glue four cookies on cup and remaining cookies on place mat.

Napkin Rings

1 For each cookie, use circle punch to make one circle from cookie-print paper. Use ribbon punch to make two slits ¼ inch apart near one edge of cookie. Print name of each guest on a cookie.

2 Cut 1½ x 6-inch strip ivory card stock. Using ruler and pencil, make a mark every inch along one long edge. Use ribbon punch to make slits in center of strip at each mark.

3 Cut two ½ x 6-inch strips cookie-print paper. Glue to card stock above and below row of ribbon punches. Glue ends of strip together to form ring.

4 Thread red ribbon through slits in ring and cookie. Tie ribbon in a bow.

Place Cards

1 Print guest's name on a small piece of ivory card stock. Cut into a small rectangle.

2 Glue rectangle on piece of cookie-print paper. Cut around cookie paper, leaving a ½-inch border.

3 Cut a 2-inch square of card stock. Fold over a ½-inch tab along one edge. Glue tab to center back of place card so it will stand up.

Party Favor

Cookie Bouquet

1 Paint outside of flowerpot white. Let dry. Repeat.

2 Cut a ½-inch-wide strip of cookie-print paper long enough to go around rim and overlapping ½ inch. Glue paper to flowerpot rim.

3 Decorate flowerpot with red and yellow paint. Let dry.

4 Place half of plastic foam ball in top of flowerpot, flat side up.

5 Spread a thin layer of glue over plastic foam. Sprinkle with red sugar crystals. Let dry.

6 Using toothpick, poke fairly large hole in stuffing in edge of sandwich cookie. Gently push end of lollipop stick into hole. Be careful not to break cookie.

7 Cut five pieces of licorice. Use toothpick to poke smaller holes in stuffing. Use toothpick to gently push ends of licorice strings into holes.

8 Place tip on frosting can. Decorate fronts and sides of cookies. Add candies, using frosting as "glue." Use frosting to repair any loose sticks or licorice strings. Lay cookies flat to dry.

9 Insert ends of cookie stems carefully into plastic foam in pot. Give one cookie flower to each of your guests when they leave.

Cookie Pizza

1 Preheat oven to 350 degrees.

2 Press cookie dough into a pizza pan. Have guests add their favorite toppings—coconut, chocolate chips, M&M's and other candies.

3 Ask an adult to help you bake cookie pizza in oven for 15 minutes or until dough is lightly browned. Let cool.

4 Have guests help decorate cookie pizza using cans of frosting with decorator tips.

5 Use pizza cutter to cut cookie pizza into wedges. Serve your yummy pizza to your guests!

Things You'll Need

* Cookie dough

Note: Mix up a double batch of chocolate-chip cookie dough ahead of time or buy prepared cookie dough.

* Round pizza pan
* Pizza cutter
* Toppings: chocolate chips, M&M's, coconut, chopped nuts, marshmallows
* Cans of white frosting with decorator tips
* Spatula

▶CONTINUED FROM PAGE 37

7 Print party information onto ivory card stock using felt-tip pen or computer. Trim card stock with scissors to measure 3¼ x 4¼ inches. Glue to front of invitation.

8 Trim one short end of striped paper with wavy scissors. Glue to opposite end of card, overlapping top of ivory card stock.

9 Fill cellophane bag half-full of cookies. Fold over end of bag and insert between layers of card stock at 1-inch line, tucking in front of invitation at the same time. Staple through all layers.

Food Fun!

Offer your guests glasses of icy-cold *Marbleized Milk* to go with your delicious Cookie Pizzas. The recipe is on page 171.

Fairy Dance Party

You and your friends can all be fairy princesses! Dance to music, make fantasy favors and eat fun food made especially for your enchanted friends.

By Koren Russell

Fairy Dust Invitation

1 Photocopy invitation (page 175) onto white card stock.

2 Trim invitation to measure 4 x 5¼ inches.

3 Fill in blanks on invitation with silver pen. Let dry.

4 Lay tulle rectangle on top of invitation. Glue tulle to invitation with tiny dots of glue in each corner. Let dry.

Things You'll Need
* White card stock
* 4 x 5¼-inch piece white tulle with silver sparkles
* Metallic silver pen
* Photocopier
* Clear-drying craft glue
* Scissors
* Ruler

Invitation
  Fairy Dust Invitation
Decorations
  Fantasy Table Covering
  Twinkle Lights
Party Favors
  Fairy Wand
  Fairy Dance Memory
   Book
Activities
  Fairy Gown Contest
  Fairy Dance
Food Fun
  Mini PB & Honey
   Sandwiches*
  Mini Fruit & Dip*
  Tiny Cupcakes*
  Dainty Sugar Cookies*

Look for these recipes in the Food Fun chapter, pages 142–173. You'll find lots of EXTRA food ideas to choose from!

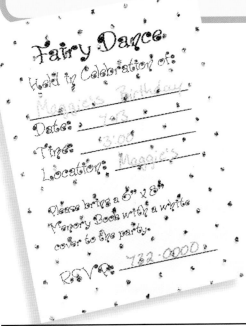

Fairy Dance
Held in Celebration of:
Maggie's Birthday
Date: 7/8
Time: 3:00
Location: Maggie's

Please bring a 6" x 8" Memory Book with a white cover to the party.
RSVP 732-0000

Fantasy Table Covering

Things You'll Need

* White tablecloth
* White tulle slightly larger than top of table
* ¼-inch curling or metallic ribbon: pink, silver and lavender
* White lights
* Silver star garland

1 Cover table with tablecloth. Arrange white lights on tablecloth in a loose circle. Scatter lengths of looped ribbon and strands of silver star garland around table.

2 Drape tulle lightly over lights, ribbon and garland.

Twinkle Lights

Hang tiny white Christmas lights around the room. Put them on "twinkle" setting. Wrap 6-inch-wide strips of tulle around lights.

42

Fairy Wand

1 Cut 18 inches from each piece of wire. Hold wires together with ends even. Thread 3 inches of the wire through a bead.

2 Push pointed end of kabob stick into bead from other side. Push stick in firmly so that point sticks out other side. Bend long ends of wire off to one side. Use wire cutter to cut off point of stick.

3 Twist wires around and around each other.

4 Bend wire ½ inch from bead to form a 1-inch circle. Twist circle twice. Bend circle to the left. Leave ½ inch of space and form another circle, twisting it twice. Leave ½ inch of space and form a third circle, twisting it twice. Bend circle to the right.

5 Cut off wires, leaving ¾-inch-long ends.

6 Gently pull bead and wires off stick. Thread all wire ends back through same side of bead. Push stick back through other side of bead, pushing it in as far as possible. If bead doesn't fit tightly, add a drop of glue.

7 Twist 3-inch wire ends together. Wrap them around stick three times, right below bead. Trim off extra with wire cutters. Use pliers to push wire ends against stick.

8 Place center of tulle square over other end of stick. Slide other bead onto end of stick, over tulle.

9 Hold remaining 4-inch pieces of wire together and twist together. Wrap them around stick, just above bead, three times. Trim off extra wire with wire cutters. Use pliers to push wire ends against stick.

10 If desired, decorate wand with long lengths of silver ribbon.

Things You'll Need

* Wooden kabob stick
* 2 (12mm) round wooden beads
* 2-inch square white tulle with silver sparkles
* 22 inches 20-gauge wire: silver and purple
* Clear-drying craft glue
* Ruler
* Wire cutters
* Pliers

Fairy Dance Memory Book

Things You'll Need

★ 6 x 8-inch spiral-bound memory book with white cover
★ 4¼ x 5½-inch decorative papers—at least 3 colors, in solids and prints
★ Plain white paper
★ 3 x 7-inch white tulle with silver sparkles
★ 5 silver daisies
★ Metallic silver pen
★ Pencil
★ Glue stick
★ Clear-drying craft glue
★ Scissors
★ Ruler

1 Cut a 4¼-inch square from blue paper. Glue to cover on diagonal using glue stick.

2 Trace patterns (page 178) onto plain white paper. Cut out.

3 Trace around fairy head and body on wrong side of print paper. Trace around wing on wrong side of purple paper. Flip wing pattern over and trace around it a second time. Cut out all pieces.

4 Trace another pair of wings onto wrong side of tulle. Cut out.

5 Arrange head, body and paper wings on cover. Glue paper wings to cover with glue stick.

6 Lay tulle wings over paper wings. Glue tulle wings to cover using just a dot of clear-drying glue at points of wings.

7 Glue head, body and silver daisies to cover with craft glue.

8 For name tag, cut ¾ x 1¾-inch piece of purple paper. Print name with silver pen. Let dry.

9 Cut 2¼ x 1¼-inch piece tulle. Apply craft glue to back of name tag. Press over tulle. Glue tag on cover.

10 Glue ½-inch-wide strips of tulle across top and bottom of cover, using small dots of clear-drying glue on each end.

Fairy Gown Contest

1 Divide your guests into teams of two each. Set a timer for 7 minutes.

2 Have one member of each team dress the other in a "fairy gown," using only a roll of bathroom tissue.

3 Use applause to choose the "Most Creative" and "Funniest" gowns. Award the prizes.

Things You'll Need
* 1 roll of bathroom tissue for each two guests
* Timer
* Four prizes

Fairy Dance

Play a magical fairy version of Musical Chairs! Set up chairs in a circle so there is one less chair than there are guests. Play music and everyone must dance and twirl like fairies until the music stops. Whoever doesn't find a chair is out of the game. Play music and remove one chair each time until only one fairy is left. Choose music like *Dance of the Sugarplum Fairies*.

Food Fun!

Tiny treats make fun refreshments for this party! Check out the directions for *Mini PB & Honey Sandwiches*, *Mini Fruit & Dip*, *Tiny Cupcakes* and *Dainty Sugar Cookies*. Look for these recipes on pages 142–173.

Ballet Dance Party

Celebrate with your friends who love to dance. Whether it's ballet, tap, jazz or rock, you'll have a ball!

By Sharon Reinhart

Invitations
"Admit One" Ticket

Decorations
Beaded Napkin Rings
Beaded Place Cards

Party Favors
Ballet Bear

Activities
Paperclay Pin/Magnet
"Design A Dance
    Costume" Bookmark
"My First Pointe Shoes"
    Holder

Food Fun
Sugared Ballet Slipper
Cookies*

*Look for this recipe in the Food Fun chapter, pages 142–173. You'll find lots of EXTRA food ideas to choose from!

LET'S HA

"Admit One" Ticket

1 Lay ivory card stock on worktable so that longer edges run from left to right.

2 Lay ruler across card stock, near top. Measure 5½ inches in from left edge and mark a dot very lightly. Move ruler near bottom of card stock. Very lightly, make another tiny dot 5½ inches from left edge.

3 Line up ruler along dots you made in step 2. Fit paper trimmer with scoring blade. Carefully run blade along ruler to score card stock from top to bottom. (If you don't have a paper trimmer with scoring blade, use a stylus or a dry ballpoint pen to score the line.) Fold card in half.

4 Using the circle punch, punch two half-circles on each side of card, at center.

5 Using the same method in steps 2 and 3, score a line over card stock from top to bottom, 1 inch from left edge, and a second line 1 inch from right edge.

6 Open card and lay face up on foam pad. Using needle and ruler (for measuring), carefully poke a tiny hole through card on scored line, 1/16 inch from edge. Poke a hole every 1/8 inch along scored line. Repeat along second scored line.

7 Use glue stick to glue green striped paper in center of card front. (Stripes should run up and down.)

8 Press on alphabet stickers along one line to spell "ADMIT." On line below, press on stickers to spell "ONE." *Tip: Use a needle or pin to remove stickers from sheet.*

9 Using markers, calligraphy pens or computer, print desired wording onto cream card stock. Trim printed card stock to measure 3½ x 1¾ inches.

10 Using same method as in steps 2 and 3, score two lines over card stock, one 5/8 inch from left edge and one 5/8 inch from right edge.

11 Use darning needle to poke holes along both scored lines as in step 6.

12 Glue printed cream card stock to sage green card stock at an angle. Glue card stock inside card at an angle.

Things You'll Need

* 3¾ x 11-inch piece ivory card stock
* 3¾ x 11-inch piece cream card stock
* 4¼ x 2½-inch piece sage green card stock
* 3½ x 3¾-inch piece green striped scrapbooking paper (stripes should run up and down)
* 1¼-inch circle paper punch
* Gold alphabet stickers
* Scissors or paper trimmer with cutting and scoring blades
* Dry ballpoint pen or stylus
* Darning needle, nail or ice pick
* Foam pad, like mouse pad or craft foam
* Ruler
* Glue stick
* Double-sided tape
* Markers, calligraphy pens or computer with printer

"Scoring"

means making a crease in paper so it will fold evenly.

Place a ruler along a line you want to fold, then use a tool such as a dry ballpoint pen, stylus, or the tip of a letter opener to gently make a crease in the paper. Be careful not to tear the paper.

Beaded Napkin Rings

1 Have an adult remove shanks from buttons.

2 Using tacky glue or hot glue, glue button to metal piece on elastic ring. Let glue set.

3 **Option**: String alphabet beads on pink 26-gauge wire to spell out each guest's name. Fill the wire with 5mm pony beads. Twist wire ends together to make a ring. Clip off extra wire. Slide ring over napkin.

Things You'll Need
For each napkin ring:
* ✶ Pastel covered elastic hair bands
* ✶ Ballet theme buttons
* ✶ Wire cutters or craft nippers
* ✶ Tacky glue or hot-glue gun
* ✶ Alphabet beads
* ✶ 26-gauge wire

Beaded Place Cards

1 Fold card stock in half to measure 1½ x 2½ inches.

2 Spell out name with alphabet beads. Attach beads to front of card with glue dots.

3 Add sticker at each end of name.

4 Peel backing from magnet. Press inside place card, behind name. After the party, your guests can cut off the back of the place card and use the front for a personalized magnet!

Things You'll Need
For each place card:
* ✶ 3 x 2½-inch piece sage green card stock
* ✶ Ballet slippers stickers
* ✶ Alphabet beads in assorted colors
* ✶ Mini glue dots
* ✶ 1-inch piece adhesive-backed magnet

 Food Fun! Serve *Sugared Ballet Slipper Cookies* to your guests. Look for this recipe on page 159.

Ballet Bear

1 Use tape measure to measure around bear's waist. Add ½ to 1 inch to this measurement. Then cut a piece of each gathered lace to fit.

2 Glue 1¾-inch lace around bear's waist, overlapping ends in back. Glue ¾-inch lace over 1¾-inch lace.

Things You'll Need
* Jointed craft bear
* Gathered lace, 1¾ inches and ¾ inch wide
* 2 white satin mini bows
* Fabric glue
* Tape measure

3 Cut a piece of ¾-inch lace long enough to go around bear's neck and cross over in front, as shown. Glue at front of bear.

4 Glue one white bow by bear's ear. Glue other bow to front of bear as shown.

Things You'll Need
For each pin or magnet:
* Paperclay
* 1¾-inch round or scalloped cookie or clay cutter
* Rolling pin to use with paperclay or straight-sided glass
* Rubber stamp with dance motto*
* Orchid ink pad
* Violet/gold craft paint
* Small flat paintbrush
* Purple mulberry paper
* Adhesive pin back or magnet
* Clear-drying glue
* Waxed paper

*PSX rubber stamp (#D3123) was used to make this project.

Paperclay Pin/Magnet

Before Your Party

1 Roll clay ⅛ inch thick on waxed paper.

2 Press stamp onto orchid ink pad. Stamp motto onto clay once for each pin or magnet.

3 Cut out with cookie cutter. Let dry.

Let's Begin!

1 Paint stamped clay with light coat of violet/gold paint. Let dry.

2 Tear several small pieces of mulberry paper. Glue to back of clay as shown.

3 Attach pin or magnet to back.

"Design a Dance Costume" Bookmark

Before Your Party

Trace all the patterns (page 178) onto scraps of cardboard or card stock and cut out for your guests to use.

Let's Begin!

1 Trim two corners from sage green card stock to make it look like a large tag, as shown.

2 Using scissors, cut a 3 x 5-inch piece from pink print or green print paper. Glue tag onto right side of paper. Trim paper edges with paper edgers. Punch hole in center of notched end of tag.

3 Fold ribbon in half. Poke looped end of ribbon through hole in tag. Thread ribbon ends through ribbon loop and tighten to attach ribbon to tag.

4 Thread ribbon ends through pony bead. Push bead down to edge of tag. Glue in place with clear-drying glue.

5 Trace pattern(s) for dance costume of your choice (page 178) onto wrong side of pink, pearl and green papers; cut out.

6 Glue costume pieces together with glue stick. If you like, decorate costume with dots of glitter glue, ribbon bows, etc.

7 Glue mini hanger to back of costume with 3-D foam. Attach small pieces of 3-D foam to back of costume in center and on skirt. Press costume onto tag at an angle.

Things You'll Need

For each bookmark:

* 2½ x 4¾-inch piece sage green card stock
* Scrapbooking papers: pearl pink, pink print and green print
* Scraps of card stock or cardboard
* Pearlized pink 5mm pony bead
* 9 inches pink or willow green ⅛-inch satin ribbon
* Miniature wire clothes hanger, 1⅜ x 1 inch
* Crystal glitter glue
* Paper edgers with sunflower pattern
* Oval paper punch
* Glue stick
* Double-sided tape
* 3D adhesive foam squares
* Clear-drying craft glue

"My First Pointe Shoes" Holder

 Cover mirror with masking tape to keep paint off it.

 Paint front and back of mirror frame with two coats pink paint. Let paint dry between coats. Don't forget the edges of the frame.

 Remove masking tape. Clean mirror, if needed. If you like, trim photo to fit over mirror. Glue photo in place.

 Plan layout of stickers and rhinestone transfer. Refer to the photo. Note that the shoes will hang down the left side of frame.

 Arrange stickers to spell "My First Pointe Shoes" or other lettering. Press stickers firmly into place.

 Following directions on package, have an adult help you iron the rhinestone transfer in bottom right corner of frame.

 With an adult's help, use an iron and the press sheet to iron a silver heart at each corner of center opening.

 Brush front of frame with one coat of varnish, keeping it off of the mirror/photo. Let dry.

Things You'll Need

For each holder:
* 10-inch square wood-framed mirror
* Pink acrylic craft paint
* Matte-finish craft varnish
* Foam paintbrushes
* Rhinestone ballet shoes transfer*
* 4 silver ⅜-inch iron-on hearts
* Teflon press sheet
* Iron
* Silver 1-inch alphabet stickers
* White cup hook
* Painter's masking tape
* Photo (optional)

*Creative Crystals Rhinestone Ballet Transfer (#HFM121) was used to make this project.

Penguin Party

You don't have to go to Antarctica for an icy *brrrrthday* party! Friends can dress up in their black and white duds and slide on over. This party is cool—really cool!

By Helen Rafson

Invitation
"Brrrrthday Party!"
Decorations
Penguin Table Decorations
Deep Sea Table Covering
Party Favors
Place-Card Frame
Goody Bag
Activities
Penguin Party Game
Penguin Visors
Food Fun
South Pole Snacks*
Penguin Tuna Sandwiches*
Deep Sea Gelatin*
Icy-Cold Fruit Juice*
Penguin Cupcakes*

*Look for these recipes in the Food Fun chapter, pages 142–173. You'll find lots of EXTRA food ideas to choose from!

Perky Penguin

Follow these directions for making penguins to use for your invitations, napkin rings, ornaments, place cards and goody bags.

Cut It Out

1 Trace patterns for penguin body, penguin wing, penguin beak, feet and penguin face/hat (page 179) onto white paper. Cut out.

2 Trace patterns on poster board as follows: black—one body, two wings; orange—one beak, two feet; white—one face; red—one hat. Cut out.
Optional: Punch two 1-inch orange

Things You'll Need
For each penguin:
* Poster board: black, orange, red and white
* White paper
* 2 black 6mm half-round beads
* ½-inch red glitter pompom or ⅜-inch red button for invitations only
* 2 white ¼-inch buttons
* 10 inches ⅜-inch red grosgrain ribbon
* Black fine-tip marker
* White gel pen or fine-tip opaque marker
* Paper punches*: 1-inch and 1¼-inch hearts (optional)
* Clear-drying craft glue
* Pencil
* Ruler
* Scissors

*McGill Inc. Super Giant (#88111) and Giant (#91200) heart punches were used to make these projects.

▶CONTINUED ON PAGE 55

"Brrrrthday Party!"

Perky Penguin

1 Make Perky Penguin *except* do not glue pompom to hat. Instead, thread needle with embroidery floss. Insert needle in one hole of button and out the other. Tie floss in a knot.

2 Cut end to ⅜-inch length. Use the point of a pin to separate the strands of floss to "fluff them up." Glue button to tip of hat with craft glue.

Lettering & Frames

1 Print party information onto white paper using felt-tip pen or computer. Trim paper with scissors to measure 4½ x 2½ inches. **Option:** *Trace or photocopy party information (page 180) onto plain white paper.* Fill in the blanks.

2 Glue white paper to snowflake paper. Use ruler and pencil to draw a ¾-inch-wide border frame on snowflake paper. Cut out. Glue to inside of card.

3 Print and frame "Brrrrthday Party!" in the same way as party information. Glue to front of card.

4 Use black marker to draw a dashed line around outside edge of white paper.

5 Glue Perky Penguin to bottom left corner of card.

Things You'll Need

For each invitation:

* Perky Penguin (see instructions on page 52)
* 5 x 7-inch white card with envelope
* Snowflake-print paper
* White paper
* 6-inch piece of red embroidery floss
* Embroidery needle
* ⅜-inch red two-hole button
* Pin
* Felt-tip pens, gel pens *or* photocopier
* Black fine-point marker
* Scissors
* Ruler
* Clear-drying craft glue
* Glue stick

Penguin Table Decorations

Things You'll Need

For each napkin ring:

* Perky Penguin (see instructions on page 52)
* 1¼-inch-wide ring cut from the cardboard tube inside bathroom tissue
* Black craft paint
* Paintbrush
* Clear-drying craft glue

Penguin Napkin Rings

1 Paint cardboard ring black, inside and out. Let dry. Paint again.

2 Glue penguin to ring.

3 Fold or roll napkin. Slide ring over napkin.

Penguin Cups

1 Trace patterns for penguin face/hat, feet, cup wing and cup beak (page 179) onto white paper. Cut out.

2 Trace patterns onto poster board as follows: black—two cup wings; orange—one cup beak, two penguin feet; white—one penguin face/hat. Cut out. *Optional: Punch two 1-inch orange hearts for feet. Punch one 1¼-inch white heart for face.*

Things You'll Need

For each cup:

* Black drinking cup
* Poster board: black, orange, red *and* white
* White paper
* 2 (6mm) half-round black beads
* 2 (12mm) wiggly eyes
* 15 inches ⅝-inch red grosgrain ribbon
* Black fine-tip marker
* White gel pen or fine-tipped opaque marker
* Paper punches*: 1-inch and 1¼-inch heart (optional)
* Clear-drying craft glue
* Pencil
* Ruler
* Scissors

*McGill Inc. Super Giant (#88111) and Giant (#91200) heart punches were used to make this project.

Add Some Details

1 Draw a dashed line around edge of white face and orange feet with black marker.

2 For nostrils, draw two short lines on orange beak with the black pen.

3 Draw a dashed line around edges of black wings with white gel pen or opaque marker.

Put It All Together

1 See photo and glue white face, beak and eyes to cup.

2 Glue feet to the bottom of the cup.

3 Glue middle of ribbon to center back of cup. Tie ribbon in a bow on center front of cup. Cut ends at a slant.

4 Glue wings to sides of cup.

Perky Penguin

▶ CONTINUED FROM PAGE 52

hearts for feet. Punch one 1¼-inch white heart for face. Punch one 1¼-inch red heart for hat.

 Cut off rounded edges of red heart along dashed line.

Add Some Details

1 Draw a thin line around edge of hat with black marker. Draw a line across the top of the brim. Draw "ribbing" lines in brim.

 Draw a dashed line around edges of white face and orange feet with black marker.

 For nostrils, draw two short lines on orange beak with the black pen. (Don't draw the dashed fold line.)

 Draw a dashed line around edges of black wings with white gel pen or opaque marker.

Put It All Together

1 Fold the beak in half. Glue bottom of beak to face. For eyes, glue black half-round beads to face just above beak.

2 See photo and glue face and hat to body.

3 Glue points of feet to back of body. Glue buttons to center front of body.

4 Glue middle of ribbon to center back of body. Tie ribbon in a bow on center front of body. Cut ends at a slant.

5 Glue wings to front of penguin. Glue pompom to tip of hat.
Note: For invitations only, glue button on instead of pompom. See invitation instructions steps 1–2.

Deep Sea Table Covering

Let's Begin!

Lay tablecloth on table. Sprinkle with snowflake spangles.

Things You'll Need
★ Blue tablecloth
★ Silver snowflake spangles

Note: If you can't find snowflake spangles, use a snowflake paper punch to make flakes from silver card stock.

Goody Bag

1 Use black marker to draw a dashed line around edges of bag.

2 Cut a 3⅝ x 4⅞-inch piece of snowflake paper. Glue to center front of bag with glue stick.

3 Glue penguin to center of bag with craft glue.

4 Tie ribbon in a bow around one handle of bag. Cut ends at a slant.

Things You'll Need

For each goody bag:
* Perky Penguin (see instructions on page 52)
* 4 x 5¼-inch white gift bag
* Snowflake-print paper
* 15½ inches of ⅝-inch red grosgrain ribbon
* Scissors
* Black fine-tip marker
* Pencil
* Ruler
* Glue stick
* Clear-drying craft glue

Place-Card Frame

Things You'll Need

For each place-card frame:
* Perky Penguin (see instructions on page 52)
* 6 x 4-inch horizontal acrylic frame White card stock
* Photo to fit in frame
* Snowflake-print paper
* Silver snowflake spangle
* Black fine-tip marker
* Scissors
* Ruler

1 Cut 3 x 5-inch rectangle from white card stock.

2 Glue white card stock to snowflake paper. Use ruler and pencil to draw a 1-inch wide border frame on snowflake paper. Cut out.

3 Draw a dashed line on outside edge of card stock. Print or write name of guest on card stock.

4 Glue snowflake spangle to card stock. Insert piece inside frame. Glue penguin to front of frame.

5 At your party, take a group photo of all your guests. Later, give one to each guest to put in her frame as a keepsake of the coolest party ever!

Penguin Party Game

1 Give each guest pencil and paper. Set the timer for 3 minutes.

2 Let guests see how many words they can make using only the letters in the word *penguin*. You can use two n's because there are two in *penguin*. Use the other letters only once.

3 Award the prize.

Answers: pen, pin, pine, nine, pig, in, gin, ping, nun, pun, gun, pug, nip, I, up

Penguin Visors

Before Your Party

Trace and cut out the pieces for each guest's visor. Then they will only need to add details with a marker and glue everything together.

If you have time at your party, your guests can cut their own pieces. Photocopy or trace enough patterns for everyone. Have plenty of pens, scissors and glue bottles.

Let's Begin!

1 Trace patterns for visor face, visor cheek, visor heart and visor beak (page 179) onto white paper. Cut out.

2 Trace patterns on craft foam as follows: white—one face, two hearts; orange—beak; pink—two cheeks. Cut out. **Optional:** *Punch two white hearts instead of cutting them.*

3 Use marker to draw a dashed line around edges of cheeks and beak. Draw a dot-dash line along top and sides of face. Draw two straight lines for nostrils on beak.

4 Glue face to visor. Trim bottom edge even with visor if needed. Glue cheeks, beak and eyes to face. Glue one small heart to each cheek.

Things You'll Need

For each visor:
* Black plastic visor
* Craft foam: white, orange and pink
* White paper
* 2 (28mm) wiggly eyes
* Black fine-tip marker
* Small heart paper punch* (optional)
* Craft glue
* Scissors
* Pencil
* Photocopier (optional)

*A Fiskars small heart punch was used to make this project.

Food Fun! Serve *South Pole Snacks, Penguin Tuna Sandwiches, Deep Sea Gelatin* and *Penguin Cupcakes*. Wash it all down with *Icy-Cold Fruit Juice*. See pages 142–173 for recipes and ideas.

"Pamper Yourself Silly" Slumber Party

You'll have the silliest, most wonderful time of your life when you make and use your own spa products! Fun activities will make you and your friends giggle into the night.

By Jill DeAnn Evans

Invitation
  Come to the Silly Spa!
Decorations
  Make a Spa!
Party Favors
  Silly Spa Delights
Activities
  Spa "Beauty Treatments"
  Lotions & Potions
Food Fun
  Tortilla Pinwheels*
  Chocolate-Dipped
    Strawberries*
  Cheese and Crackers
  Fresh Fruits and
    Vegetables
  Sparkling Fruit Drinks

Look for these recipes in the Food Fun chapter, pages 142–173. You'll find lots of EXTRA food ideas to choose from!

Invitation

Come to the Silly Spa!

1 Trim both sheets of white paper to measure 3½ x 10 inches.

2 Use your computer or pens to print the invitation's front page on one piece. Start writing 3 inches from the top edge:

> You are cordially invited
> To
> PAMPER YOURSELF SILLY!
> At the
> (your last name)
> Slumber Spa Party

3 On the second sheet, print the information for inside the invitation. Start 1 inch from the top, and fill in the blanks:

Make a Spa!

Spas are peaceful places where people relax. To make your party room look like a spa, try this:

★ Roll up lots of fluffy towels. Put them in a big basket.

★ Set ferns, flowers and other plants around the room.

★ Pile up pretty pillows.

★ Set up beach chairs or patio chairs. Drape towels over them.

★ Ask an adult to set up a tabletop fountain.

★ Fix a tray with a pitcher and glasses of ice-cold water or lemonade. Put a slice of lemon in each glass to make it pretty.

★ Play relaxing music or a CD of nature sounds.

Address:
Date & Time:
RSVP to Spa Director at (your phone number) by (date you need to know if she's coming).

 4 Lay lilac card stock on work table with short edges at top and bottom. Fold in half from left to right. This makes a tall, narrow card.

 5 Glue the white cover page in the center of the mint card stock. Punch square holes along top and bottom. Glue this piece to front of lilac card.

 6 Glue silk leaves and flower to front. Press smiley sticker in center of flower.

7 Glue inside page of white paper inside invitation.

 8 Wrap ribbon around invitation. Tie it in a bow.

Things You'll Need
* ★ 2 (3½ x 10½-inch) pieces plain white paper
* ★ 8½ x 11-inch piece lilac card stock
* ★ 3⅞ x 10½-inch piece mint green card stock
* ★ Small pink or purple silk flower with leaves
* ★ Small smiley face reward sticker
* ★ Square hand punch
* ★ 16-inch piece of lilac ⅛-inch-wide satin ribbon
* ★ Computer with printer, calligraphy pens or felt-tip pens
* ★ Paper glue
* ★ Scissors

Spa "Beauty Treatments"

Give your guests "beauty treatments" during your party. Set up a "station" for each one. Have your guests take turns visiting each station. Ask family members to play along and give the treatments. It's really fun when they talk with a foreign accent and act like the staff at a real spa!

Collect everything you need for each station on a tray or rolling cart. Here are some ideas for "beauty treatments."

Scalp Massage
Gently massage your guest's head. Pretend to "read her mind" with your fingers. Remember—keep it funny and silly.

Hand Massage
Massage your guest's hands with lotion. Pretend to read her palms as you do. Tell her a silly fortune.

Baby Those Big Toes
Buy a tube of green facial mask gel or crème at the store. Follow the directions, but use it on your guest's feet. Give extra attention to those big toes!

Paint Nails
Take turns painting each other's fingernails and toenails. Add nail decals if you like.

Lotions & Potions

You and your guests can make your own flavored lip balm, lotion and beauty soap. Follow our directions here. You can find little tubes and jars at stores that sell organizing supplies. Or, buy the supplies in a kit at your craft store. Follow the kit's instructions.

Always have an adult help you melt wax or soap in the microwave.

Silly Spa Delights

Let your guests take home the lip balm, lotion and soaps they make at your party. Other ideas for favors are:

* Small pumice stone
* Nail file
* Emery board
* Nail brush
* Small bottle of nail polish
* Nail decals

Things You'll Need

* Pyrex measuring cup with lip for pouring
* Wooden craft stick for stirring
* Little tube or jar for each guest*
* Beeswax beads*
* Sunflower oil*
* Coloring powder of your choice*
* Flavoring and scent of your choice*
* Plastic pipette for transferring hot balm into tubes*

*Life of the Party products were used for this project.

Lip Balm

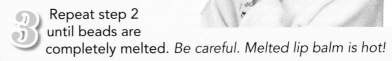

1. Pour beeswax beads and oil into measuring cup.

2. Put cup in microwave. Heat for 30 seconds. Take cup out of microwave. Stir with craft stick.

3. Repeat step 2 until beads are completely melted. *Be careful. Melted lip balm is hot!*

4. Stir in flavoring one drop at a time. Stop when it smells good to you.

5. Stir in coloring powder a little at a time, until you like the color.

6. Use plastic pipette to fill tube or jar with lip balm. Be careful—it is still hot. Fill tube or jar to the rim.

Note: If the pipette clogs, squeeze it between your fingers to push out the lip balm.

7. When the tubes are filled, let them set for a few minutes. Then add a drop more of lip balm.

8. Let the tubes set for 20–30 minutes. Put on lids.

Note: If lip balm gets hard, put it back in the microwave. Heat for 30 seconds, then stir it. Repeat until it is melted again.

Lotion

1. Fill bottle half-full with lotion base.

2. Add scent and color until it smells good and looks pretty. Make it a little darker than you want. Then you won't need to add color later.

3. Put the lid on the bottle. Shake well.

4. Add lotion base until bottle is full. Shake again.

Things You'll Need

* Shea butter body lotion base*
* Lotion bottle with cap for each guest*
* Coloring powder of your choice*
* Scent of your choice*

*Life of the Party products were used for this project.

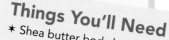

Soap

1 Ask an adult to help you cut the soap base into four equal chunks. Cut one of those pieces into little pieces. They should be no bigger than 1 inch.

2 Put the soap pieces in the measuring cup. Put cup in microwave. Heat for 30 seconds. Take cup out of microwave. Stir with craft stick.

3 Repeat step 2 until soap pieces are completely melted. *Be careful. Melted soap is hot!*

4 Stir in fragrance one drop at a time. Stop when it smells the way you want it to.

5 Stir in liquid coloring a little at a time. Stop when it looks the way you want it to.

Things You'll Need
* Pyrex measuring cup with lip for pouring
* Wooden craft stick for stirring
* 1 pound solid white soap base*
* Coloring liquid of your choice*
* Scent of your choice*
* Soap molds*
* Washable tray

*Life of the Party products were used for this project.

6 Set soap molds on a tray. Pour melted soap into molds.

7 Let molds set to cool and harden. Set a timer for 15–20 minutes. Check soap when the timer goes off. If it is solid, gently push soaps out of molds.

Fun Facts!

Did you know the skin is the body's largest organ?

It is almost waterproof. It keeps important fluids from escaping.

Skin keeps bacteria and chemicals from entering most parts of the body.

It protects your body from the sun's rays.

The skin helps keep your body temperature normal. When you get hot, it sweats to help you cool off.

There are many nerve endings in the skin. They let you feel cold and heat, pain, pressure and touch.

Your skin is one of the most important parts of your body. Treat it well!

Serve *Tortilla Pinwheels* and Chocolate-Dipped Strawberries to your guests. See pages 142–173 for this recipe, plus other great food ideas.

Food Fun!

Glamour Girl Party

Have fun dressing up like glamorous Hollywood stars! You and your friends can imagine what it would be like to be famous—even if it's just for an afternoon!

By Lorine Mason

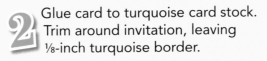
Invitation

Glamour Girl Invitation

Things You'll Need

* 7¼ x 5¼-inch white envelope
* Card stock: fuchsia, turquoise
* Black fine-tip marker
* Paper punches: oval, purse
* Double-sided tape
* Scissors
* Pencil
* Glue stick
* Tacky glue
* Ruler
* Paper trimmer (optional)
* Computer with printer (optional)

1 For card, use marker to print party information on a 6¼ x 4½-inch piece of fuchsia card stock. **Option:** *Use a computer to print words.*

2 Glue card to turquoise card stock. Trim around invitation, leaving ⅛-inch turquoise border.

3 Cut a strip of turquoise card stock ³⁄₁₆ x 5¼ inches. Glue down left side on front of envelope.

4 Punch two ovals from fuchsia card stock and one oval from turquoise. Punch a purse in the center of one turquoise and one fuchsia oval.

5 Glue punched fuchsia oval over turquoise stripe at an angle.

6 On back of envelope, glue plain fuchsia oval to center of flap. Glue punched turquoise oval slightly below fuchsia oval.

Invitation
  Glamour Girl Invitation
Decorations
  Glamorous Party Table
Party Favors
  Purse Goody Bag
Activities
  Glamour Girl
    Appointments
Food Fun
  Glamour Cookies*
  Pink Champagne*
  Chocolate-Dipped
    Strawberries*

Look for these recipes in the Food Fun chapter, pages 142-173. You'll find lots of EXTRA food ideas to choose from!

Aundrea's Glamour Salon
204 Winnipeg Street
(000) 123-4567
Your next appointment is scheduled for:
Saturday, May 10th
1:00 p.m.
Be prepared for a fun afternoon filled with pampering, games and delightful food. Please let us know if you are unable to keep your appointment.

Things You'll Need

* White tablecloth to fit table
* Paper plates, plastic champagne glasses or goblets, napkins
* 6-inch-wide gold tulle ribbon
* White marabou feather boas
* Card stock: fuchsia, turquoise
* Paper punches: oval, purse and ⅛-inch circle
* Gold star garland
* Pins
* Scissors
* Ruler

Glamorous Party Table

Table

1 Cover table with tablecloth.

2 Drape tulle around center of table. Hold in place with pins.

3 Wrap marabou boas around tulle. Hide ends on back of tulle. Hold in place with pins.

4 Punch ovals from turquoise and fuchsia card stock. Punch purses in ovals. Scatter ovals across top of table.

Glass Charms

1 Punch ovals from turquoise and fuchsia card stock. Punch purses in ovals. Make one for each glass.

2 Cut a 12-inch piece of star garland for each glass. Wrap it around glass stem.

3 Punch a small hole in top of punched oval. Thread star garland end through hole.

Napkin Rings

1 Punch ovals from turquoise and fuchsia card stock. Punch purses in ovals. Make two for each ring.

2 Cut 12-inch piece of star garland for each ring. Wrap it around a 1½-inch-diameter round glue bottle or similar object. Twist ends together. Slide ring off bottle. Curl garland ends.

3 Punch a small hole in top of each punched oval. Thread star garland end through hole.

Purse Goody Bag

Things You'll Need

* Card stock: fuchsia, turquoise
* Flat buttons: 3/8-inch purple; 1/2-inch pink
* Letter opener or stylus (optional)
* Double-sided tape
* Goodies for purse: nail polish, nail files, small jewelry-making kit, tissue packages, sunglasses, bright scarf, jewelry-themed candy, etc.
* Scissors
* Pencil
* Tacky glue
* Ruler

1 For purse flap, measure and cut one piece of fuchsia card stock 8½ x 5 inches. Lay card stock on worktable so longer edges are at top and bottom.

2 Using a ruler and letter opener, score a line across top of card stock ½ inch from top. Score

3 another line 1 inch from top. (See dashed lines on Fig. 1.)

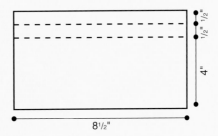

Fig. 1

For body of purse, cut an 8½ x 11-inch piece from fuchsia card stock. Lay card stock on worktable so shorter edges are at top and bottom.

4 Score a line across card stock 5 inches from top. Score another line 5½ inches from top. (See dashed lines on Fig. 2.)

5 Score a line from top to bottom, 1½ inches from left edge. Score another line 1½ inches from right edge.

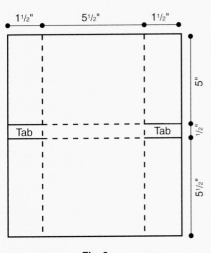

Fig. 2

▶ CONTINUED ON PAGE 66

Food Fun! Ooh-la-lah! Serve delicious *Glamour Cookies* with make-believe *Pink Champagne* and elegant *Chocolate-Dipped Strawberries*. The recipes can be found on pages 142–173.

Purse Goody Bag

►CONTINUED FROM PAGE 65

6 Cut tabs, cutting along horizontal scored lines from sides of purse to vertical scored lines. (See solid lines on Fig. 2 on page 65.)

7 For straps and bow, cut two ½ x 12-inch strips from turquoise card stock. For closing tab, cut one 1 x 3 inch piece.

8 Put double-sided tape on side tabs on body of purse. Fold tabs toward center.

9 Remove backing from tape. Fold purse along scored lines, sticking tabs to purse as purse closes.

10 Put double-sided tape on wrong side of purse flap near top edge. Stick onto back of purse body so flap folds over top and comes down front of purse.

11 Use double-sided tape to attach ends of strap to purse.

12 Fold other strip into a bow (use photo as a guide). Cut ends of bow in a "v." Attach bow and tab to front of purse with double-sided tape.

13 Glue buttons to bow and tab of purse. Fill purse with goodies.

Glamour Girl Appointments

Ask an older sister, baby sitter or parent to serve as manicurist. During the party, let each guest have an "appointment" to have her nails done. Set aside a special area with nail trimmer, buffer, a few colors of polish from which to choose, cotton balls, etc.

Let's Get Crafty Party

Set out plenty of beads, rhinestones, paints brushes, and glue! You and your friends will have so much fun making treasure boxes and notebooks that you'll want to have a crafty party every month.

By Sandy Rollinger

Things You'll Need

For each invitation:
* 3 x 5-inch white card with envelope
* Card stock: yellow, blue, purple, orange, pink, green
* Die-cut paper squares with decorative edges* (optional)
* Small star sequins
* Small rhinestones
* Pink opaque dimensional paint for paper
* Decorative paper edgers: heartstrings
* Black fine-tip permanent marker
* Toothpick
* Glue stick
* Craft glue
* Computer with printer (optional)
* Scissors
* Ruler
* Pencil

*Colorbök Square Stax paper squares were used for this project.

Invitation

"Let's Get Crafty!"

1 Use glue stick to glue six die-cut paper squares to front of card. **Option:** Cut six 1½-inch squares from card stock with decorative-edge scissors.

2 Use marker to print "SURPRISE! IT'S A LET'S GET CRAFTY PARTY," printing each word on a different color of card stock. Words should contrast with squares on invitation. Cut different shapes around words with regular scissors. **Option:** Use computer to print words.

3 Glue words onto colored squares with glue stick. Draw a wiggly line around each word with dimensional paper paint. Let dry for about 10 minutes.

▶CONTINUED ON PAGE 68

Invitation
"Let's Get Crafty!"
Decorations
Stars & Daisies
Party Favors
Notebook
Activities
Treasure Box
Food Fun
Sandwich Faces*
Fruit Kabobs*
Twinkie Centipedes*

*Look for these recipes in the Food Fun chapter, pages 142-173. You'll find lots of EXTRA food ideas to choose from!

"Let's Get Crafty!"

▶ CONTINUED FROM PAGE 67

Invitation

4 Use toothpick to put a dot of craft glue on the backs of sequins and rhinestones. Glue to invitation.

5 Use marker to print party information on yellow paper. Cut a rectangle around words with heartstrings scissors. Glue information to inside of invitation using glue stick.

PARTY IS AT _____
ADDRESS _____ HOUSE
PHONE _____
DATE _____
TIME: FROM _____ TO _____
PLEASE BRING AN APRON OR
OLD SHIRT AND LOTS OF
CREATIVITY

Decorations

Stars & Daisies

Things You'll Need
* Colored paper
* Fishing line

1 Cut out large daisies or stars and hang them from the ceiling with fishing line. Be sure to ask an adult to help you hang them so you don't damage the ceiling.

2 Cut out smaller daisies or stars and scatter them on the table before you set the table with plates, cups, and silverware.

Notebook

Things You'll Need

For each notebook:

★ 4 x 6-inch notebook
★ Polymer clay*: light blue pearl, silver
★ Alphabet clay cutters or cookie cutters
★ Star-shape clay cutters or cookie cutters in 3 sizes
★ Old rolling pin, wooden dowel or roller for polymer clay
★ Decoupage medium
★ Craft brush
★ Small star rhinestones
★ Clear fine glitter
★ Freezer paper
★ Masking tape
★ Toothpicks
★ Baking sheet lined with baking parchment
★ Oven
★ Pot holders
★ Cooling rack
★ Ruler
★ Craft glue

*Polyform Super Sculpey III clay was used for this project.

1 Tape freezer paper over top of worktable with masking tape.

2 Condition clay until it is soft and easy to form by kneading each color with your fingers and rolling it out on freezer paper with a rolling pin.

3 Roll blue clay ¼ inch thick. Use alphabet cutters to cut names or initials from clay. Place on parchment-lined baking sheet.

4 Roll silver clay ¼ inch thick. Use star cutters to cut stars from clay. Place on parchment-lined baking sheet.

5 Ask an adult to help when using the oven. Preheat oven, following directions on package of modeling compound. Bake as directed.

6 Remove hot baking sheet from oven, using pot holders. Set baking sheet on cooling rack. Let pieces cool.

7 Lay baked letters and stars on freezer paper. Brush decoupage medium over front of each piece. While still wet, sprinkle with glitter. Turn pieces over and tap off excess glitter. Let letters and stars dry.

8 Glue rhinestone star in center of each clay star. Glue clay stars and letters onto front of notebook. Let dry before using.

Food Fun! You and your friends can get crafty in the kitchen with these fun recipes! You'll love making and eating *Sandwich Faces*, *Fruit Kabobs* and *Twinkie Centipedes*! Check pages 142-173 for these recipes and lots more!

Things You'll Need

For each box:

* 4-inch square papier-mâché box with lid
* Polymer clay*: purple, yellow
* Daisy flower clay cutters or cookie cutters in 3 sizes
* Old rolling pin, wooden dowel or roller for polymer clay
* Craft paint*: copper, pearl blue, pearl violet
* Yellow opaque dimensional paint for paper
* Paintbrushes
* Small jar of water
* Star sequins, small rhinestones, etc., in different colors and shapes
* 5 (16mm) wooden beads
* Freezer paper
* Masking tape
* Paper towels
* Small glass or jar
* Baking sheet lined with baking parchment
* Pot holders
* Cooling rack
* Toothpicks
* Pencil
* Ruler
* Craft glue

* Polyform Super Sculpey III clay and Jacquard Lumiere paints were used for this project.

Treasure Box

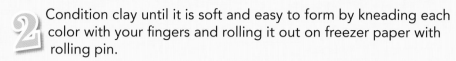

Form & Bake Flowers

1 Tape freezer paper over top of work table with masking tape.

2 Condition clay until it is soft and easy to form by kneading each color with your fingers and rolling it out on freezer paper with rolling pin.

3 Roll yellow clay ¼ inch thick. Use smallest flower cutter to cut four daisies from clay. Place on parchment-lined baking sheet.

4 Roll purple clay ¼ inch thick. Use next largest flower cutter to cut four daisies from clay. Place one yellow daisy in center of each purple one. Set flowers on parchment-lined baking sheet.

5 To make flowers for top of box, from rolled yellow clay, cut one daisy using middle-size cutter. From purple clay, cut one daisy using largest cutter. Place yellow daisy on top of purple one. Set on baking sheet.

6 Ask an adult to help when using the oven. Preheat oven, following directions on package of modeling compound. Bake as directed.

7 Remove hot baking sheet from oven, using pot holders. Set baking sheet on cooling rack. Let pieces cool.

Paint the Treasure Box

1 Using a ruler and pencil, make mark on side of box ½ inch from bottom edge. Repeat on all sides. Connect marks, drawing a straight line around the box.

2 To make a band around box, repeat step one to draw a second line around box ¼ inch above the first.

3 Paint band on box and edge of lid copper. Let dry. Add a second coat of paint, if needed. Let dry.

4 Paint top area of box and top of lid pearl violet. Paint bottom of box pearl blue. Let dry.

5 Use a pencil to trace around a small glass or bottle to make a circle in center of box lid. Paint circle pearl blue. Paint another coat of pearl blue on bottom of box. Let dry.

6 Use yellow dimensional paint to draw squiggle lines around circle and edges on lid and edges of copper band on box. Let dry.

7 Paint inside of box and lid copper. Let dry.

Put It All Together

1 Paint one bead pearl blue. Let dry.

2 Glue bead in center of one larger flower. Glue rhinestone on top of bead. Glue larger flower to lid in center of circle.

3 For feet, paint four beads pearl violet. Let dry. Glue one bead onto bottom of box at each corner.

4 Using a toothpick, put glue on back of rhinestones. Glue one in center of each smaller clay flower.

5 Lay box flat on its side. Glue one smaller daisy in center of side that is facing up. Let dry.

6 Repeat step 5 to glue a small daisy in center of each side. Let glue dry before turning box to next side.

7 Put lid on box. Using a toothpick, put glue on back of rhinestones, sequins or other decorations. Glue them onto box as you wish.

"Let's Get Crafty" Party Tips

Important: Anything used to cut or roll clay must never be used again for food preparation. Store these items in your craft area for use with clay projects.

Have extra aprons or old T-shirts on hand to cover clothing in case someone forgets to bring one.

Have plenty of baby wipes for wiping sticky hands and removing paint from fingers.

Have the table ready with freezer paper taped on for work surface. Have clays ready to condition.

Cut several 5-inch pieces of 1-inch-diameter wooden dowels to use for rolling clay.

Organize supplies—rollers, paintbrushes, cutters, etc.—so your guests will know what to do first.

Put items on several lazy susans in the center of the table so everyone can reach the supplies.

Have several small jars of water on hand to clean brushes. Remind crafters to clean their brushes between colors and after finishing painting.

Fill small containers with various kinds of confetti, rhinestones and glitter. Have several small spoons on hand for sprinkling glitter.

Make the clay decorations first. While they are baking, the crafters can paint their boxes.

While the boxes are drying, have crafters wash their hands. Then serve cookies and milk or lemonade and other treats.

Option: Cut clay shapes and bake ahead of time. Your guests can paint the boxes and just glue on the baked shapes.

Soccer Girl Party

Fly your team colors proudly! This idea is perfect for a pep rally, a celebration party, or a sporty birthday party.

By Lorine Mason

Invitation
 Team Invitation
Decorations
 Streamers & Cutouts
 Soccer Spoon Toppers
Party Favors
 Stamped Pillowcases
Activities
 Soccer Volleyball
Food Fun
 Purple Milkshakes*
 Gelatin Cups*
 Hot Dogs
 Potato Chips

Look for these recipes in the Food Fun chapter, pages 142-173. You'll find lots of EXTRA food ideas to choose from!

Team Invitation

1 For card, cut a 6½ x 4¼-inch rectangle from purple card stock.

2 Cut 4½-inch triangle of soccer paper. Glue in bottom corner of purple rectangle.

3 Cut ½-inch strip of black paper. Glue along one edge of soccer paper. Trim even with edges of card.

4 Use marker to print soccer team's name on white card stock. Cut out and glue to black card stock. Trim, leaving ¼-inch black border. Glue to front of card. **Option:** *Use computer to print words.*

5 Use marker to print party information on white card stock. Cut a rectangle around words and glue to purple card stock. Trim, leaving ¼-inch purple border. Glue inside card.

6 Press grass and soccer ball stickers along bottom edge inside card.

7 Cut 2-inch square of purple card stock and ½-inch strip of black card stock. Glue purple square over black stripe in bottom corner of envelope. Press grass and soccer ball stickers to square.

Invitation

Things You'll Need
* Card stock: purple, black, white
* Soccer ball print paper
* Stickers*: soccer balls, grass
* Scissors
* Black fine-tip marker
* Pencil
* Ruler
* Paper trimmer (optional)
* Glue stick
* Computer with printer (optional)

Frances Meyer Inc. grass stickers and Provo Craft soccer ball stickers were used for this project.

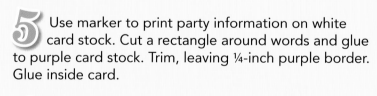

Herndon Hornets
Youth Soccer

Streamers & Cutouts

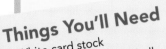

Things You'll Need
* White card stock
* Foam stamps*: soccer ball, swirly lines
* Acrylic craft paints: black, purple
* Paper clips
* Sponges
* Scissors
* ⅛-inch round hole punch
* Tacks or poster putty

*Rubber Stampede foam stamps were used for this project.

1 Using a sponge, dab black paint onto the ball stamp and purple paint onto the swirly stamp. Press stamps onto white card stock. Repeat as often as you want. Let dry.

2 Cut out around stamped designs. Use hole punch to make a hole near top edge of each cutout.

3 Thread a paper clip through each hole. Slide paper clip onto end of crepe-paper streamer. Hang streamers from walls, doorways or ceiling using tacks or poster putty.

Soccer Spoon Toppers

For Each Spoon:

1 Cut two 1½-inch squares from purple card stock.

2 Press grass and soccer ball stickers on one square. Glue squares together back-to-back, sandwiching end of spoon handle between them.

Things You'll Need
* Purple card stock
* Soccer ball stickers*
* Scissors
* Pencil
* Ruler
* Craft glue
* Plastic spoon

*Provo Craft StickyPix soccer ball stickers were used for this project.

Stamped Pillowcases

Things You'll Need

For each pillowcase:

* White pillowcase
* Foam stamps: soccer ball, swirly lines
* Acrylic craft paints: black, purple
* Fabric-painting medium
* Foam plates
* Black fabric marker
* Cardboard, size of pillowcase
* Sponges
* Scissors

*Rubber Stampede foam stamps were used for this project.

1 Put cardboard inside pillowcase to keep paint from bleeding through.

2 Mix each color of paint with fabric-painting medium on foam plate.

3 Use sponge to put black paint on soccer ball stamp. Press soccer ball stamp along border of pillowcase. Stamp several soccer balls on scrap paper.

4 While paint dries, cut out stamped paper soccer balls, leaving a ¼-inch border.

5 When paint is dry, cover stamped soccer balls on pillowcase with paper cutouts to protect them for step 6.

6 Use sponge to put purple paint on swirly stamp. Stamp swirls across border of pillowcase, over paper cutouts. Remove cutouts to reveal soccer balls underneath. Let dry.

7 Using fabric marker, write team member's name and number on pillowcase. Have guests autograph each other's pillowcases.

8 Remove cardboard from inside of pillowcase. Ask an adult to help you heat-set the paints, following the paint manufacturer's directions.

Activities

Soccer Volleyball

Use an inflatable soccer ball to play volleyball.

Food Fun!

Playing soccer is one way to work up a great appetite! Cool off with wild and wacky *Purple Milkshakes* and smooth, refreshing *Gelatin Cups*. The recipes and other fun food ideas are on pages 142–173.

Swim Party

Flip-flops, sunglasses and water make for summer fun! Be sure to bring your camera to capture all the excitement!

By Lorine Mason

Invitation

Splish Splash Invitation

Things You'll Need

★ Card stock: light, medium and dark blue; pale and bright yellow
★ 6½ x 4¾-inch envelope
★ Black fine-tip marker or computer with printer (optional)
★ Stickers: flip-flops, blue splashes
★ Scissors
★ Pencil
★ Ruler
★ Glue stick

1 Cut a 6¼ x 4½-inch rectangle from dark blue card stock.

2 Cut 1½ x 6¼-inch strip pale yellow card stock. Glue across bottom of dark blue rectangle.

3 From each color of blue card stock, cut 1½-inch-wide strip. Tear each along one long edge. Glue strips in layers on front of card to look like waves. Trim off extra paper along sides.

4 Use marker to print party information on pale yellow card stock. *Option: Use computer and printer to print words.* Trim to fit on back of dark blue card. Glue in place.

5 Cut sun and rays from bright yellow card stock. Glue to front of card.

6 Press flip-flop and splash stickers on bottom corners of card.

7 Cut 2-inch square of blue card stock. Tear along all edges. Glue to bottom corner of envelope. Press two flip-flop stickers to square.

Invitation
  Splish Splash Invitation
Decorations
  Splish Splash Napkin Rings
  Indoor Beach
Party Favors
  Goody Beach Bag
Activities
  Flip-Flops & Sunglasses
  Treasure Hunt
Food Fun
  Flip-Flop Crispy Cakes*
  Fruit Punch*

Look for these recipes in the Food Fun chapter. pages 142-173. You'll find lots of EXTRA food ideas to choose from!

Sunglasses, Swimming and Flip-Flops
Join the Fun!
Saturday, July 1st
1:00 - 4:00
Delaney's House
123 Chantel Avenue
Splish Splash

Splish Splash Napkin Rings

Let's Begin!

Cut a 1½ x 6½-inch strip from blue card stock. Press splash sticker to center of strip. Press flip-flop sticker to center of splash. Tape ends together to form a ring.

Things You'll Need

* Blue card stock
* Stickers: flip-flops, blue splashes
* Scissors
* Pencil
* Ruler
* Tape

Indoor Beach

1 Cover your party table with a light blue table cover. Add darker blue paper plates and cups. Insert blue napkins inside your Splish Splash Napkin Rings (above).

2 Add small blow-up pool toys, palm trees, etc. You can also blow up beach balls, swim rings and other pool toys, and hang them from ceilings and doorways with clear thread.

3 Drape beach towels all around, or tack them to the walls for extra color.

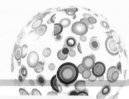

Goody Beach Bag

1 See photo and make holes along the top of the bag with hole punch, spacing 2 holes 1½ inches apart. Space each pair of holes 2 inches apart.

2 Begin at center front. Thread ribbon through holes, adding three beads to ribbon between each pair of holes. Tie ends of ribbon in a bow on front of bag.

3 Trace patterns for flip-flops (page 181) onto white paper. Trace flip-flop sole on orange foam. Trace sole on yellow foam. Cut out. Cut a ½-inch x 7-inch stip from orange foam for flip-flop strap. Glue yellow sole to orange one. Glue strap to yellow sole. Glue flip-flop to front of bag.

4 Glue foam flowers on bag. Glue a bead to center of each small flower.

Things You'll Need

For each beach bag:
* Paper bag with handle
* Craft foam: yellow, orange
* Craft foam flower cutouts: yellow, fuchsia
* White paper
* 36 inches ⅛-inch-wide orange ribbon
* Pony beads: 15 yellow, 15 orange
* ¼-inch circle hole punch
* Scissors
* Pencil
* Ruler
* Glue stick

Flip-Flops & Sunglasses

Things You'll Need

For each pair of flip-flops & sunglasses:

* ✹ Flip-flop sandals (1 pair per guest)
* ✹ Sunglasses (1 pair per guest)
* ✹ Multicolored stringy yarn
* ✹ Craft foam flower cutouts: fuchsia, pink and green gingham
* ✹ ½-inch purple buttons
* ✹ Large needle or skewer
* ✹ Scissors
* ✹ Pencil
* ✹ Ruler
* ✹ Craft glue
* ✹ Glue stick

Flip-Flops

 1 Cut a 5-yard piece of yarn. Tie one end around strap of flip-flop, near sole. Add a drop of glue to end of yarn. Poke end of yarn into sole using a needle or skewer.

 2 Wrap yarn around the strap, forming a loop. Thread remaining yarn through loop and pull tight. Repeat to cover entire thong.

 3 At other end, tie a knot and trim off extra yarn. Add a drop of glue to end of yarn. Poke end of yarn into sole using a needle or skewer.

 4 Glue craft-foam cutouts and buttons to top of strap.

Sunglasses

Glue foam cutouts and buttons to sunglasses however you wish. Make sure you can still see through the lenses.

Treasure Hunt

Let's Begin!

Turn on lights on treasure chest toys. Throw them into the pool. Let guests take turns diving in and collecting as many chests as they can before lights stop blinking.

Things You'll Need
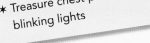
* ✹ Treasure chest pool toys with blinking lights

Another Idea: Scavenger Hunt

Toss a number of things into the pool and have your friends dive in to collect items. The winner is the one who finds the most items.

 Food Fun! Cool off with *Flip-Flop Crispy Cakes* and refreshing *Fruit Punch*. Look for these recipes on pages 142–173.

Scrapbooking Party

Invite your friends to join in the fun of scrapbooking! You'll love decorating album pages that show off a photo. Make little pockets to hold secret notes from each other.

Note: *Instructions are given for tracing and cutting out patterns, but a paper trimmer, die cuts and punches can also be used.*

By Julie Stephani

Invitation
  Scrapbooking Party
  Invitations
Decorations
  Flower Table Decorations
Party Favors
  Scrapbook Goody Bags
Activities
  "4 Ever Friends" Pages
Food Fun
  Mini Pizza Pies*
  Ice-Cream Shakes*

*Look for these recipes in the Food Fun chapter, pages 142-173. You'll find lots of EXTRA food ideas to choose from!

Scrapbooking Party Invitations

1 Cover worktable with tablecloth or plastic bags.

2 For card, cut 5 x 8-inch rectangle of yellow card stock. Fold in half to measure 5 x 4 inches. Trim bottom edges of card with seagull scissors.

3 Use marker or computer to print inside information on 3 x 3¾-inch white paper. Cut out with scissors. Glue onto turquoise paper. Trim around edges with ripple scissors, leaving a ¼-inch turquoise border. Glue inside card.

▶ CONTINUED ON PAGE 83

Invitations

Things You'll Need
* Waterproof tablecloth or plastic trash bags
* Plain brightly colored paper or card stock: yellow, pink, purple, turquoise, orange, green
* Plain white paper
* 6 x 4⅜-inch white envelopes
* Daisy die cuts*: 1 large (3-inch) and 1 small (2-inch) for each invitation (optional)
* Black fine-tip marker or computer with printer
* Dimensional foam dots
* ¼-inch circle punch
* Circle punches*: 1-inch and ½-inch (optional)
* Decorative-edge scissors*: seagull, ripple
* Scissors
* Pencil
* Ruler
* Glue stick

*These products were used in this project: Sizzix die-cutting machine and dies; Fiskars trimmer and scissors; Marvy Uchida punches.

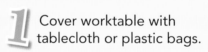

Things You'll Need

* Waterproof tablecloth or plastic bags
* Large and small napkins
* Plastic cups
* Brightly colored paper or card stock: pink, purple, turquoise, orange, yellow, green
* Small (2-inch) daisy die-cut* for each napkin, napkin ring and cup (optional)
* ½-inch circle punch* (optional)
* Fine-tip black marker
* Decorative-edge scissors*: ripple
* Scissors
* Pencil
* Ruler
* Glue stick

*These products were used in this project: Sizzix die-cutting machine and dies; Fiskars trimmer and scissors; Marvy Uchida punches.

Flower Table

Let's Begin!

Cover worktable with a tablecloth or plastic bags.

Flowers

 For each flower, trace one small flower (page 182) onto colored paper and one small circle (page 182) onto yellow. Cut out with scissors. *Option: Use flower die cut and punch center with circle punch.* Glue circle in center of flower.

2 Use marker to draw eyes and smiling mouth.

Small Napkins

1 Make as many flowers as you need to decorate one napkin for each guest.

 Glue one flower in corner of each napkin.

Napkin Rings

1 Make as many flowers as you need to decorate one napkin ring for each guest.

2 For each ring, cut 1 x 6-inch strip green paper with ripple scissors. Bend strip into a circle, overlapping ends. Glue ends together. Glue flower on center front of ring.

3 Fold large napkin and slip ring over top.

Cups

1 Make as many flowers as you need to decorate one cup for each guest.

2 For each cup, cut one 2 x ¾-inch strip colored paper using ripple scissors. Print name of friend on strip with marker.

3 For stem, cut one ⅛ x 2-inch strip from green paper. Glue one end to back of flower. Glue flower to cup. Glue name strip over bottom of stem.

Scrapbook Goody Bags

Things You'll Need

For each bag:
- ✶ Waterproof tablecloth or plastic bags
- ✶ Small brightly colored paper gift bag
- ✶ Paper tissue
- ✶ Brightly colored paper or card stock: pink, purple, turquoise, pink, yellow
- ✶ Large (3-inch) daisy die cut* for each goody bag (optional)
- ✶ 1-inch circle punch* (optional)
- ✶ Black felt-tip marker
- ✶ Pencil
- ✶ Scissors

*These products were used in this project: Sizzix die-cutting machine and dies; Fiskars trimmer and scissors; Marvy Uchida punches.

1 Cover worktable with a tablecloth or plastic bags.

2 For each bag, trace one large flower (page 182) onto bright color of paper and one large circle (page 182) onto yellow. Cut out with scissors. **Option:** *Use flower die-cut and punch center with circle punch.* Glue circle in center of flower.

3 Use marker to draw eyes and smiling mouth.

4 Glue flower to bag. Fill bag with paper tissue and scrapbooking supplies.

Food Fun!

Your friends will love mixing ingredients and flavors to make *Mini Pizza Pies* and *Ice-Cream Shakes*. Find the recipes and lots of other fun food ideas on pages 142–173.

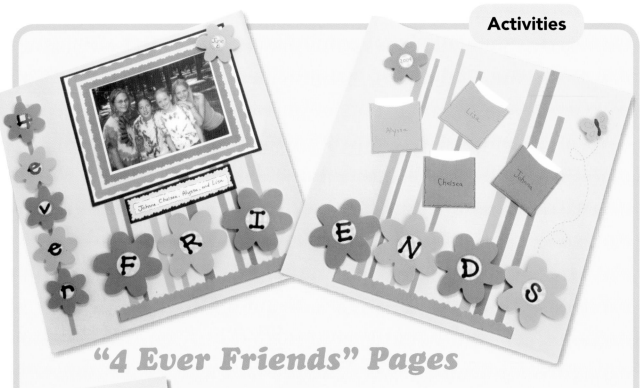

"4 Ever Friends" Pages

Things You'll Need

For each guest:
★ Waterproof tablecloth or plastic bags
★ 2 yellow 12 x 12-inch paper sheets (for pages)
★ Plain, brightly colored paper or card stock: pink, purple, turquoise, orange, gold, green
★ Plain white paper
★ 2 clear 12 x 12-inch plastic protective sleeves
★ Black felt-tip marker
★ Dimensional dots
★ Die cuts*: 7 large (3-inch) daisies and 7 small (2-inch) daisies, 1 (1¼-inch) butterfly (optional)
★ Black 1-inch letter stickers (optional)
★ Circle punches*: 1-inch and 9/16-inch (optional)
★ Decorative-edge scissors*: seagull, ripple, peaks
★ Scissors
★ Pencil
★ Ruler
★ Glue stick

*These products were used in this project: Sizzix die-cutting machine and dies; Fiskars trimmer and scissors; Marvy Uchida punches.

Before Your Party

Make sample pages for your friends to use as a guide.

Prepare the Pieces

1 Cover worktable with a tablecloth or plastic bags.

2 Trace seven large flowers and seven small flowers (page 182) onto different colors of paper *except* yellow. Trace one butterfly (page 182) onto pink paper. Trace seven large and seven small circles (page 182) onto yellow paper. Cut out with scissors.
Option: *Use flower and butterfly die cuts and punch centers with circle punches. Glue circle in center of each flower.*

3 For stripes, cut 16 (11-inch) strips of different widths (¼–7/16 inch) from any color except yellow.

4 For grass, cut two ¾ x 8-inch strips from green paper. Cut along one long edge with peaks scissors.

5 Trace one pocket (page 182) for each guest onto assorted bright colors of paper *except* yellow. If you have four guests, trace four pockets. Cut out with scissors.

6 Fold pockets in half. Open pockets and put a thin

▶ **CONTINUED ON PAGE 82**

"4 Ever Friends" Pages

▶CONTINUED FROM PAGE 81

line of glue along each side edge. Fold pockets closed again. Press together along sides.

7 To make layered frame for the party photo, cut 4 x 6¼-inch rectangle white paper. Glue onto purple paper. Cut around it with ripple scissors, leaving ⅜-inch purple border.

8 Repeat step 7 to add more layers and borders—first yellow, then green, white and black. Trim edges with seagull scissors and regular scissors.

9 For name caption, print names of friends in photo on ½-inch-wide strip of white paper. Cut it as long as needed. Glue it onto yellow paper. Cut around it with ripple scissors, leaving a ³⁄₁₆-inch yellow border. Glue it onto black paper. Cut around it with regular scissors, leaving a ⅛-inch black border.

Put It All Together

1 Arrange all pieces on 12 x 12-inch pages. Follow the photo, or place pieces however you like.

2 Press letter stickers onto flowers as shown. Spell out "4 ever" on small flowers and "FRIENDS" on large ones. *Option: Print number and letters on flowers with marker.*

3 Use marker to write month and day of party on one small flower and year on another. Outline butterfly wings and color body.

4 Glue stripes first. Glue one green stripe down left side of left-hand page so that it is centered behind "4 ever" flowers. Cut remaining strips in different lengths before gluing them.

5 Glue grass, photo frame, name caption and pockets to pages.

6 Peel paper off one dimensional dot. Press it onto center back of flower. Repeat on each flower and butterfly. Press flowers and butterfly onto pages.

7 With marker, draw squiggly outline with slash marks around name caption, and down sides and across bottom of grass and pockets.

8 With pencil, draw butterfly's loopy "flight path." Use marker to trace dashed line over penciled line. Erase pencil marks.

9 For notes, cut 1¾ x 2⅜-inch rectangles from white paper, one for each pocket. Have guests write short notes to each other. Put them in pockets. Use marker to write the name of the person who wrote the note on each pocket.

Make Kits for Your Guests

It's a good idea to prepare some of the materials for making the scrapbook pages before your guests arrive. Then you and your friends will have more time for the really fun part—decorating your pages!

Put enough supplies for each person in one plastic bag. Follow our suggestions here for what to do ahead of time. Place the rest of the supplies on the table for everyone to share.

In each guest's kit, include:

- One 4¼ x 6¼-inch paper rectangle. Have your guests use this to plan where to put the party photo on the page. (Label it "Photo" with a marker if you want.) Take a picture of all of your friends at the party. Afterward, have copies made and give one to each guest to add to her scrapbook pages. **Option:** *Take instant photos at the party.*
- *Stripes:* Sixteen 11-inch paper strips, ¼–⁷⁄₁₆ inch wide, cut from five assorted bright colors.
- *Grass:* Two ¾ x 8-inch strips green paper.
- *Flowers:* Seven large flowers and seven small ones cut from a mixture of brightly colored papers.
- *Flower centers:* Seven large circles and seven small ones cut from yellow paper.
- *Butterfly:* One butterfly cut from pink paper.
- *Pockets:* If you have four people at your party, include four pockets in each kit. Cut them from a mixture of brightly colored papers.
- **Notes:** One 1¾ x 2⅜-inch piece of white paper for each pocket.

Option: *For larger parties, set up different workstations. For example, have the punches at one station, paper trimmer or decorative-edge scissors at another, etc.*

Invitations

Scrapbooking Party Invitations

▶ CONTINUED FROM PAGE 78

4 Referring to patterns on page 182, use pencil to trace one large flower on orange paper, one small flower on blue, and one large circle and one small circle on yellow. Cut out with scissors. **Option:** *Use flower die cuts and circle punches.* Glue circles in center of flowers. Use marker to draw eyes and smiling mouths.

5 For cheeks, cut or punvh two tiny circles from pink. Glue to large flower at ends of mouth. Peel paper off one dimensional dot and press on center back of large flower. Press flower on center of card, leaving enough room below flower for printing.

6 Cut three ⅛-inch-wide strips of colored paper, 2¾–3¼ inches long. Glue two to left side and one to right side of large flower.

7 Using marker, draw squiggly outline with slash marks around flower. Print "It's A Scrapbooking Party!" below flower.

8 On envelope, use marker to draw squiggly outline with slash marks around edges of envelope. Glue small flower in top right corner.

9 With a pencil, draw stem and leaves. Use marker to draw dashed line over stem and trace solid lines over leaves. Add dashed lines down center of leaves. Erase pencil lines.

Pony Party

Round up your friends for some Western fun! Be ready for lots of horsing around!

By Sandy Rollinger

Invitation
Pony Invitation

Decorations
Pony Party Lights
Western Tableware
Western Place Mats
Western Cups

Party Favors
Western Visors
Pony Pens

Activities
Pony Bingo

Food Fun
Ho Ho Ponies*
Marbleized Milk*

Look for these recipes in the Food Fun chapter, pages 142–173. You'll find lots of EXTRA food ideas to choose from!

Invitation

Pony Invitation

Pony Head

1 Trace the pattern for the invitation pony (page 183) onto white paper. Cut out.

2 Trace pony onto tan parchment. Cut out. Erase pencil lines.

3 Draw outlines and nostrils with blue paper paint. Let dry for 15 minutes.

Invitation Cover

1 Cut a piece of blue card stock 4¼ x 2¾ inches. Cut

▶ CONTINUED ON PAGE 89

Things You'll Need
For each invitation:
* Waterproof tablecloth or plastic trash bags
* White 5 x 3-inch invitation card
* Matching envelope
* Card stock: red, blue
* Tan parchment paper
* White paper
* Burlap
* Sky blue paper paint
* Buttons: 2 (⅝-inch) flat red, ½-inch flat blue
* 6mm wiggly eye
* Black fine-tip marker
* Decorative-edge scissors: mini scallop
* Glue stick
* Craft glue
* Scissors
* Pencil
* Eraser
* Ruler
* Computer with printer (optional)

*Plaid Enterprises provided the paint for paper for this project.

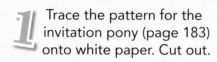
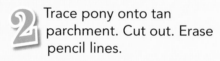

PLEASE COME TO MY PONY PARTY

PLACE..............
DATE..............
TIME..............
PHONE..............

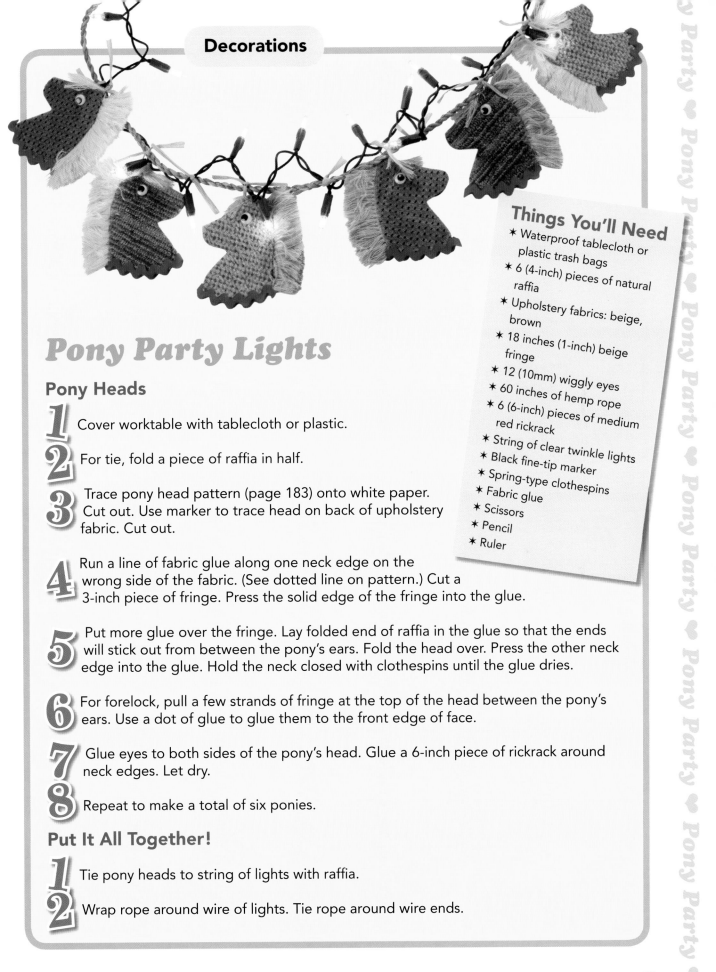

Things You'll Need
* Waterproof tablecloth or plastic trash bags
* 6 (4-inch) pieces of natural raffia
* Upholstery fabrics: beige, brown
* 18 inches (1-inch) beige fringe
* 12 (10mm) wiggly eyes
* 60 inches of hemp rope
* 6 (6-inch) pieces of medium red rickrack
* String of clear twinkle lights
* Black fine-tip marker
* Spring-type clothespins
* Fabric glue
* Scissors
* Pencil
* Ruler

Pony Party Lights

Pony Heads

1 Cover worktable with tablecloth or plastic.

2 For tie, fold a piece of raffia in half.

3 Trace pony head pattern (page 183) onto white paper. Cut out. Use marker to trace head on back of upholstery fabric. Cut out.

4 Run a line of fabric glue along one neck edge on the wrong side of the fabric. (See dotted line on pattern.) Cut a 3-inch piece of fringe. Press the solid edge of the fringe into the glue.

5 Put more glue over the fringe. Lay folded end of raffia in the glue so that the ends will stick out from between the pony's ears. Fold the head over. Press the other neck edge into the glue. Hold the neck closed with clothespins until the glue dries.

6 For forelock, pull a few strands of fringe at the top of the head between the pony's ears. Use a dot of glue to glue them to the front edge of face.

7 Glue eyes to both sides of the pony's head. Glue a 6-inch piece of rickrack around neck edges. Let dry.

8 Repeat to make a total of six ponies.

Put It All Together!

1 Tie pony heads to string of lights with raffia.

2 Wrap rope around wire of lights. Tie rope around wire ends.

Western Tableware

1 Cut a 2½-inch-wide ring from cardboard tube. Measure and cut a 3-inch-wide strip of denim long enough to go around the cardboard ring and overlap ¼ inch.

2 Spread glue on outside of cardboard ring. Press denim onto it, leaving extra fabric hanging over both edges.

3 Cut a slit in the extra fabric every ½ inch, up to the cardboard ring.

4 Spread a little glue inside the ring, along the edges only. Bend the fabric tabs inside the ring and press them into the glue. Let dry for about 5 minutes.

5 Measure and cut two pieces of red rickrack long enough to go around the ring. Glue them near the top and bottom edges of the ring.

6 Wrap the raffia around the ring four times. Tie the ends in a knot on the front. Cut the raffia ends 1 inch long. Glue the button over the knot. Let dry for about 1 hour.

7 Fold the bandanna for a napkin. Place inside the ring. Arrange the fork, knife and spoon inside the ring on top of the bandanna.

Western Place Mats

1 Trim edges of craft foam with cloud scissors.

2 Pull out threads along edges of burlap to make a ½-inch-long fringe. Glue burlap in center of foam place mat.

3 Glue denim in center of burlap.

4 Cut and glue rickrack around edges of denim. Glue a red button in each corner. Let dry.

Western Cups

Things You'll Need

For each cup:
* Red plastic cup
* Blue denim fabric
* 16 inches of medium red rickrack
* ⅝-inch flat red button
* Natural raffia
* Black fine-tip marker
* Fabric glue
* Scissors
* Pencil
* Ruler

1 Measure and cut a 2-inch-wide strip of denim long enough to go around the cup and overlap ¼ inch. Glue around cup.

2 Measure and cut two pieces of red rickrack long enough to go around the cup. Glue them around the top and bottom edges of the denim.

3 Wrap the raffia around the cup four times. Tie the ends in a knot on the front of the cup. Cut the raffia ends 1 inch long. Glue the button over the knot. Let dry for about 1 hour before using.

Another Idea: Party Favor Cups

Use the cups as party favors filled with candies and a Pony Pen.

Party Favors

Western Visors

Things You'll Need

For each visor:
* Blue denim visor
* 1⅞-inch beige fur fringe*
* 12 inches of medium red rickrack
* Buttons: 3 (⅝-inch) flat red, 3 (½-inch) flat blue
* Natural raffia
* Spring-type clothespins
* Fabric glue
* Scissors
* Pencil
* Ruler

*Suedette provided Fur Fringe for this project.

1 Cut a piece of fringe long enough to fit across the front of the visor from one end of the bill to the other.

2 Run a line of glue across the front of the visor at the bottom of the headband. Press fringe into glue. Let dry.

3 Cut a piece of red rickrack the same length as the fringe. Run a line of glue onto the top edge of the fringe edge. Press rickrack into glue. Let dry.

4 Tie a bow with two 12-inch strands of raffia. Glue the bow to the front of the visor over the rickrack.

5 Glue the blue buttons over the center of the bow in a triangle. Glue a red button over the blue buttons. Glue a red button on each end of the fringe. Let dry for about 1 hour before wearing.

Pony Pens

Follow instructions for making Pony Heads for the Pony Party Lights (page 85), but do not add the raffia hangers. Place finished pony head over top of pen.

Things You'll Need

For each pen:
* Pony Head (see page 85)
* Red or blue pen

Pony Bingo

Before Your Party: Make Playing Boards

1 Cover worktable with tablecloth or plastic bags.

2 Measure and cut 5-inch squares from red and blue craft foam, one piece for each playing board. Trim edges with cloud decorative-edge scissors.

3 Use black marker to print "pony" words on red and blue card stock. (See list at right.) *Option: Use computer with printer.* Cut rectangles around words.

4 Place words on foam boards in four rows of three words each. Use red words on blue boards and blue words on red board. Mix up the words. Put different words in different places on each playing board.

Things You'll Need

For each game board:
* ★ Waterproof tablecloth or plastic trash bags
* ★ Craft foam: blue, red
* ★ Card stock: blue, yellow
* ★ Black fine-tip marker
* ★ Decorative-edge scissors: clouds
* ★ Bowl of pebbles, corn kernels, etc., to use for markers
* ★ Scissors
* ★ Craft glue
* ★ Pencil
* ★ Ruler
* ★ Computer with printer (optional)

Pony
Horseshoe
Horse
Cart
Hay
Bridle
Saddle
Reins
Carrots
Apples
Whinny
Neigh
Gallop
Trot
Jump
Canter
Mane
Tail
Barn
Stall
Trail
Hoof
Curry Brush
Spurs
Boots
Stirrups

5 Repeat steps 1–4 to make as many playing boards as you need for your guests.
Note: Be sure to place the words in different places on each card.

Words to Draw

1 Print the same "pony" words on yellow card stock. Cut rectangles around the words.
Option: Use computer to print the words on card stock before cutting them out.

To play: Put the yellow words in a bowl. Give everyone a playing board and some pebbles, corn kernels or other markers. Draw the yellow words from the bowl, one by one, and call them out. The first player to fill a line across or up and down yells "Pony Bingo!" and wins a prize.

Have plenty of small prizes available. It's not unusual for two or more to get "Pony Bingo!" at the same time. Let everyone have a chance to win!

Food Fun! *Ho Ho Ponies* and *Marbleized Milk* are sure to round up lots of giggles! Check pages 142–173 for the instructions and other great recipes for food and drink.

Pony Invitation

▶ CONTINUED FROM PAGE 84

a piece of red card stock 3⅝ x 2¼ inches. Trim edges of both pieces with mini scallop scissors.

2 Use glue stick to glue the blue and red card stock to front of the card at different angles. (See the photo.)

3 For the mane, cut a piece of burlap 1 x 2 inches. Pull out threads along one 2-inch edge to make a ½-inch-long fringe.

4 Glue the woven edge of the fringe to the back of the pony's neck so fringe sticks out. Glue the pony to the invitation.

5 Use craft glue to glue the eye onto the pony. Glue the red buttons in opposite corners of the blue card stock. Glue the blue button in the bottom left corner of the red card stock.

Inside of Invitation

1 Cut a 3 x 2¾-inch piece of parchment paper. Trim edges with mini scallop scissors.

2 Use the marker to print the party information.
Option: Use a computer to print the words before cutting the parchment.

3 Use the glue stick to glue the parchment inside the invitation.

Kitty & Puppy Party

Be as playful as a puppy or as curious as a kitten when you and your animal-loving friends get together for a party that's bow-wow wonderful and pretty purrfect!

By Sandy Rollinger

Invitation
  Kitty & Puppy Invitation
Decorations
  Carousel Centerpiece
Party Favors
  Kitty & Puppy Pops
Activities
  Pretty Patchwork Frame
  Pet Balloons
Food Fun
  Kitty Cupcakes*

Look for this recipe in the Food Fun chapter, pages 142–173. You'll find lots of EXTRA food ideas to choose from!

Kitty & Puppy Invitation

Kitty & Puppy

1 Cover worktable with tablecloth or plastic bags.

2 Cut small triangles and squares from each color of pastel paper. Trim some edges with ripple scissors.

3 Brush decoupage liquid onto front of card. Lay one layer of paper pieces in liquid. Overlap edges of pieces. Brush more decoupage liquid over paper. Add enough layers of paper pieces to cover front of card. Brush with more decoupage liquid. Let dry.

4 Trace puppy head, small tail, jumping puppy body and kitty head (pages 184 and 185) onto white paper. Cut out.

5 Trace puppy head, tail and jumping puppy body onto blue parchment.

6 Trace kitty head onto pink parchment.

7 Paint puppy ears and spots blue. Paint nose brown. Paint inside of kitty's ears fuchsia. Let dry.

8 Paint small curved line for highlight on puppy nose with 3-D white paint. Let dry.

9 Cut out kitty and puppy pieces. Cut tail off puppy body.

10 Use fine-tip marker to add dashed outlines around kitty and puppy shapes. Outline puppy's toes, nose, ears and spots with dashed lines. Add eyebrows to kitty and puppy and details to kitty ears.

11 Use medium-tip marker to draw mouths and freckles.

12 Use toothpick to apply glue on back of wiggly eyes. Glue eyes to faces.

Put It Together

1 On front of invitation in upper right corner, measure in 1 inch from top and side edges. Mark spot with pencil.

2 Ask an adult to help you make a small hole at the spot using nail or tip of sharp

Things You'll Need
For each invitation:
* Waterproof tablecloth or plastic trash bags
* 3 x 5-inch white invitation card with envelope
* Pastel print paper: yellow, blue, pink
* Parchment paper or card stock: blue, pink
* Yellow computer paper
* Plain white paper
* 4 (5mm) wiggly eyes
* Decoupage liquid
* Shimmery brush-on fabric paints: fuchsia, robin's egg blue, brown
* Shiny white 3-D craft paint
* Paintbrushes
* Nail or sharp pointed scissors
* Small eyelets: pink, blue
* Eyelet-setting tool
* Small hammer
* Wood block
* Glue stick
* Craft glue
* Decorative-edge scissors: ripple
* Regular scissors
* Toothpicks
* Black markers: fine-tip and medium-tip
* Computer with printer (optional)
* Pencil
* Ruler

▶ CONTINUED ON PAGE 92

▶ CONTINUED FROM PAGE 91

scissors. Make another hole at bottom of tail (dot on pattern).

3 Push blue eyelet through hole in tail, then through invitation. Fit eyelet end on back. Place on a wood block. Set tip of eyelet tool in eyelet. Ask an adult to help you gently tap the tool with a hammer to fasten eyelet.

4 Glue body and head onto front of invitation. Cover eyelet with body, but keep glue away from tail so it is free to "wag."

5 Use markers to print "It's a Kitty and Puppy Costume Party!" on yellow paper. *Option: Use computer and printer.* Cut around each word. Glue words across front of puppy as shown in photo.

6 Inside invitation in upper right corner, measure in 1¼ inches from top and side edges. Mark spot with pencil.

7 Ask an adult to help you make a small hole at the spot. Make another hole at kitty's nose.

8 Push a pink eyelet through nose, then through invitation. Fasten same as in step 3.

9 Use markers to print party information on yellow paper. *Option: Use computer and printer.* Cut rectangle around words with ripple scissors. Glue inside invitation with glue stick, sliding edge under kitty.

Carousel Centerpiece

Carousel Top & Bottom

Note: Cover worktable with tablecloth or plastic bags.

1 Cut six 1½ x 5-inch strips from each color of print paper using regular scissors.

2 Cut six 2-inch squares from each color of print paper using cloud scissors.

3 Use regular scissors to cut enough 1½-inch-wide strips of white craft foam to wrap around the edges of both foam circles.

4 Glue foam strips around foam edges, having top edges even. Trim off any extra craft foam where ends meet. Stick straight pins through the strips to hold them until glue dries.

5 Glue 5-inch paper strips over foam strips. Alternate colors. Trim off extra paper where ends meet.

6 Glue a 2-inch paper square over the 5-inch strips wherever strips meet. Use different colors.

7 Using regular scissors, trim the paper strips and squares so edges are even with the foam strips.

8 Glue the jar lid in the center of one plastic foam circle. This will be the bottom of the base. Let dry.

9 Glue yellow rickrack over paper along one edge of each circle. Glue pink rickrack over paper along other edge of each circle. Let dry.

Carousel Poles & Topper

1 *Note: Ask an adult to help when using the saw.* Cut four 7-inch pieces of dowel. Paint dowels and wooden ball yellow. Let dry.

Things You'll Need

Things You'll Need

* Waterproof tablecloth or plastic bags
* Pastel print paper: yellow, blue, pink
* Craft foam: white, pink
* 2 (10-inch) plastic foam circles, 1 inch thick
* 8½ x 11-inch sheet plain white paper
* 28 inches ¼-inch-diameter wooden dowel
* Shimmery brush-on fabric paints: fuchsia, robin's egg blue, egg yolk yellow, brown, white
* Shiny white 3-D craft paint
* Paintbrushes
* Toothpick
* ⅜- to ¾-inch flat buttons: blue, pink, white, yellow
* Rickrack: yellow, blue, pink
* 1½-inch wooden ball
* 8 (5mm) wiggly eyes
* Large plastic jar lid, 4½ inches in diameter
* Straight pins
* Tape measure
* 4 spring clothespins (optional)
* Decorative-edge scissors: cloud
* Medium-tip black permanent marker
* Small saw
* Container of water
* Paper towels
* Paper plate
* Thick craft glue
* Scissors
* Pencil
* Ruler

 Note: *You may want to ask an adult to help you figure out the math in this step.* To make marks on foam circle to show where to place the dowels, wrap tape measure around outside of the foam circle. Write down this measurement. Divide by four. Use this number to make four marks an equal distance apart for each dowel. Repeat for other foam circle.

Kitties & Puppies

1. Trace puppy head, kitty head, jumping puppy body and jumping kitty body (pages 184 and 185) onto white paper. Cut out.

2. Trace two puppy heads and two jumping puppy bodies onto white craft foam. Trace two kitty heads and two jumping kitty bodies onto pink craft foam.

▶CONTINUED ON PAGE 94

Fun & Games

Have your guests take turns naming different breeds of dogs. If someone can't name a breed when it's her turn, she is out. Keep going until only one person is left. Give the winner a prize.

Decorations

▶ CONTINUED FROM PAGE 93

3 Mix blue and white paint on a paper plate to make light blue. Do not mix it too much. You want some lighter and darker streaks. Paint puppy bodies and heads, using a sweeping motion. Let dry.

4 Paint puppy ears and spots with plain blue. Paint noses brown. Let dry.

5 Mix fuchsia and white paint. Do not mix it too much. You want some lighter and darker streaks. Paint kitty bodies and heads. Let dry.

6 Paint triangles in kitty ears with plain fuchsia. Paint noses egg yolk. Let dry.

7 Paint small curved line for highlight on each puppy and kitty nose with 3-D white paint. Let dry.

8 Cut out painted kitty and puppy pieces.

9 Using black marker, add dashed outlines around kitten and puppy shapes. Outline toes, noses and puppy ears and spots with dashed lines. Draw mouths, freckles and eyebrows.

10 Use toothpick to apply glue on back of wiggly eyes. Glue eyes to faces. Glue faces to bodies.

Put It Together

1 Use a dowel to press a hole ½ inch deep into both foam circles at each mark. **Note:** *All holes should be the same depth. Mark a line on the dowel ½ inch from end. Press dowel into the circle up to the mark.*

2 Put craft glue in holes in one foam circle for bottom of carousel. Set dowels in holes. Wipe off any glue drips. Let dry for 2 hours.

3 Cut yellow rickrack to fit around edge of bottom circle between dowels. Glue in place. Glue three buttons around each dowel. Let dry for 30 minutes.

4 Put glue in holes in other foam circle for top of carousel. Turn bottom of carousel upside down. Fit dowels into holes. **Note:** *Ask an adult to hold the top while you guide the dowels into the holes.* Wipe off any glue drips. Let dry for 2 hours.

5 Cut two blue rickrack pieces to fit across top of foam circle, making an "X." Glue in place. Cut two pink rickrack pieces to fit between blue rickrack pieces, making an "X." Glue in place. Glue yellow wooden ball in center of foam circle.

6 Glue buttons around bottom of ball. Glue buttons over ends of rickrack pieces. Glue buttons between rickrack pieces.

7 Glue kitties and puppies onto poles. Hold in place with clothespins until glue sets. Place carousel in center of table. Surround with Kitty Cupcakes (page 162).

Kitty & Puppy Pops

Kitties & Puppies

 Trace puppy head and kitty head (page 185) onto white paper. Cut out.

 Trace puppy heads onto white foam and kitty heads onto pink foam. Trace one head for each lollipop.

 Mix blue and white paint on paper plate to make light blue. Do not mix it too much. You want some lighter and darker streaks. Paint puppies. Let dry.

 Paint puppy ears and spots plain blue. Paint noses brown. Paint eyes white. Let dry.

 Mix fuchsia and white paint, but don't mix too well. Paint kitties. Let dry.

 Fill triangles in kitty ears with plain fuchsia. Paint noses egg yolk. Paint eyes white. Let dry.

 Use black marker to draw dashed outlines around heads. Outline noses, and puppy ears and spots with dashed lines. Draw mouths, freckles and eyebrows. Add details to kitty ears.

 Paint small curved lines for highlights on each puppy and kitty nose with white 3-D paint. Let dry.

 With marker, make a small black dot in each white eye.

 Cut out painted kitty and puppy pieces.

Put It Together

 Glue one head to each lollipop.

 Tie ribbon bow around lollipop stem. Cut ends at a slant.

Things You'll Need
* Craft foam: pink, white
* Shimmery brush-on fabric paints: fuchsia, robin's egg blue, egg yolk yellow, brown, white
* Shiny white 3-D craft paint
* ⅛-inch yellow satin ribbon
* Small lollipops
* Black permanent marker
* Container of water
* Paintbrushes
* Toothpick
* Paper towels
* Paper plate
* Thick craft glue
* Scissors

Food Fun! Every puppy and kitty loves special treats! Treat your guests to *Kitty Cupcakes*. Look for this and other recipes on pages 142–173, along with other fun serving tips.

Pretty Patchwork Frame

Kitty & Puppy Party ♥ Kitty & Puppy Party ♥ Kitty & Puppy Party ♥ Kitty & Puppy Party

Things You'll Need
* ★ Waterproof tablecloth or plastic bags
* ★ 8½ x 6½-inch flat wooden or papier-mâché frame
* ★ Pastel print paper: yellow, blue, pink
* ★ Decorative-edge scissors: cloud
* ★ Jumbo rickrack: yellow, pink
* ★ Paintbrush
* ★ ¾- to ⅞-inch flat buttons: 4 pink, 4 yellow
* ★ Decoupage liquid
* ★ Craft glue
* ★ Container of water
* ★ Scissors
* ★ Ruler
* ★ Pencil
* ★ Digital camera, computer and printer (optional)

1. Cover worktable with tablecloth or plastic bags. Remove glass from frame. Set glass aside.

2. Measure width of frame. Cut several strips of print paper that width and 3 inches long.

3. Lay paper strips on frame, alternating colors. Trim off any paper that hangs over the edge.

4. Glue paper pieces to frame with decoupage liquid. Smooth paper with your fingers. Brush another coat of decoupage liquid over the paper. Let dry.

5. Cut 2-inch-wide strips of assorted printed papers. Trim shorter edges with cloud scissors.

6. Brush decoupage liquid over seams on frame where paper strips meet. Lay 2-inch strips over seams.

7. Brush entire frame with one coat of decoupage liquid. Let dry.

8. Using craft glue, glue yellow rickrack around center opening. Glue pink rickrack around outer edge.

9. Glue pink buttons to inner corners. Glue yellow buttons to outer corners.

10. Take individual or group photos of your guests. Use a digital camera and computer with printer, or ask an adult to take the film to a one-hour photo shop. Before your guests leave, have your guests put the glass and photos in their frames.

Pet Balloons

1. Fill yellow, blue and pink balloons with helium. (Purchase a small, party-size helium tank at a party supply store or have the balloons filled at the store.) Tie long strands of pastel curling ribbon around knots.

2. Make puppy and kitty eyes, ears, mouths, noses and whiskers from different colors of craft foam. Glue them to the balloons. They'll look great as they float freely around the room!

Artist Party

Have you always wanted to find your artistic talents? Invite some friends over to "discover the artist within." It will be a creative adventure!

By Jill DeAnn Evans

Things You'll Need

To make 2 invitations:

* 8½ x 11-inch sheet white paper
* 8½ x 11-inch sheet black card stock
* Small pieces of colored card stock or paper: yellow, red, green, blue, purple, orange, white
* Fine-tip markers or computer with printer
* Small oval hand punch
* Glue pen or paper glue
* Scissors
* Ruler
* Pencil

Invitation

Artist's Palette

1 For each card, cut one 5½ x 8½-inch piece from black card stock. Fold piece in half to make a 5½ x 4¼-inch card.

2 For front of card, use black marker to print "You're Invited" on white card stock. Cut a 5 x 3-inch rectangle around words so that words are in upper left-hand corner. Glue on front of card.

3 For inside of card, print "To Discover the Creative Artist Within" and other party information on white paper. Cut a 5 x 3-inch rectangle around words. Glue inside card. **Option:** Print information using computer and printer.

4 Tear or cut strips and shapes of different colored paper. Glue them to front of card. **Option:** Draw decorations with markers.

▶ CONTINUED ON PAGE 98

Invitation
  Artist's Palette
Decorations
  Autographed Drop Cloth
Party Favors
  Mini Art Kits
Activities
  Edible Sculptures
  Wax-Resist Painting
Food Fun
  Painted Toast*
  Chips
  Soft Drinks
  Ice Cream

Look for this recipe in the Food Fun chapter, pages 142–173. You'll find lots of EXTRA food ideas to choose from!

Mini Art Kits

Fill small paper or fabric bags with pocket-size art supplies. Some ideas include: a small sketch pad, charcoal pencil and eraser, mini watercolor set with paintbrush, small box of crayons, pastels or chalks, miniature markers.

Artist's Palette

▶ CONTINUED FROM PAGE 97

5 Trace patterns for palette, paintbrush handle, and brush tip (page 181) onto white paper. Cut out.

6 Trace palette onto white card stock. Cut out. Using the oval punch, make a hole near the notch for the artist's "thumb hole."

7 Glue palette over the colored shapes.

8 Trace and cut a paintbrush handle from black card stock and a brush tip from orange. Tear paint puddles from different colors. Glue them to the palette. **Option:** *Color paintbrush and paints with markers.*

Other Ideas

Hang bright streamers all over the room. Hang copies or posters of famous art on the walls. Play classical music softly in the background.

Food Fun! Food makes great art! Let each guest go wild with *Painted Toast.* This recipe and other ideas can be found on pages 142–173.

Decorations

Autographed Drop Cloth

Things You'll Need
* Plastic drop cloth
* Plain fabric sheet
* Acrylic fabric paints or fabric marking pens
* Paintbrushes

1 Lay or hang plastic drop cloth to protect walls and floor. Lay or hang sheet on top of plastic.

2 Invite guests to sign, decorate and doodle on the sheet with fabric paints or fabric markers. Let dry.

3 Take a photo of everyone with the drop cloth for a great souvenir of your artistic party!

Edible Sculptures

Before Your Party

1 Wash and dry your hands.

2 Mix peanut butter, honey and dry milk powder in a large bowl. Use spoon at first, then your hands. Mash and knead dough until it is smooth and pliable. If it is too sticky, mix in more powdered milk.

3 Wrap the dough in plastic wrap or put it in an airtight container. Store it in the refrigerator until your party.

When You're Ready to Sculpt

1 Cover your worktable with clean plastic wrap. Tape in place to hold.

2 Have all your guests wash and dry their hands.

3 Give each guest a chunk of peanut butter clay. Have them try to mold a copy of a statue, a toy or some other item.

4 Let your guests decorate their "sculptures" with candies, raisins, chips or coconut.

5 Eat the sculptures right away, or put them in a plastic bag or airtight container to eat later.

Things You'll Need
* 2 cups smooth, creamy peanut butter
* 1 cup honey or light corn syrup
* 2 cups dry powdered milk
* Decorations: small candies, raisins, chocolate chips, shredded coconut
* Large paper or plastic plates
* Sculpting tools: toothpicks, butter knives, forks, spoons
* Bowl
* Wooden spoon
* Plastic wrap or airtight container
* Pictures or models of famous sculptures (optional)

Note: These amounts will make enough peanut butter clay for six guests. Increase the amounts if you have more people at your party.

Things You'll Need
* Box of 64 crayons
* Large watercolor brushes or small foam brushes
* Watercolor paint: black or dark blue
* Foam plates
* Masking tape
* 9 x 12-inch sheets white Bristol paper
* Copies of famous paintings or drawings from art books or Internet (optional)
* Scissors

Wax-Resist Painting

1 Color picture on paper with crayons. Copy a famous picture, or color your own creation. Use heavy pressure when coloring. Leave background and some areas blank. These will be filled in later with paint.

2 Tape all the drawings flat on the worktable or countertop. Use small pieces of masking tape.

3 Mix watercolor paint and water on a foam plate. Brush the paint over all the drawings. The uncolored areas will soak up the paint. Let dry.

4 Remove the tape carefully. Trim off unpainted edges with scissors. Have everyone sign his or her creations, just like an artist!

Flower Power Party

Flowers are in bloom everywhere for spring or summer parties. Make friendship daisy chains and edible flowers!

By Karen Booth

Invitation

Flower Invitation

Things You'll Need

* Pastel card stock and envelopes
* Light green card stock or construction paper
* Crayons
* Fine-point permanent black marker
* Flower rubber stamps and ink pad (optional)
* Scissors
* Pencil
* Glue stick
* Low-temperature glue gun with glue sticks
* 4-inch silk flower heads
* Compass or drinking glass

1 For each invitation, fold 4 x 8-inch card stock in half to make a square card. Trace a 4-inch circle onto front of card. The edge of the circle should touch the fold.

2 To make a hinge, do not cut the circle for 1 inch along fold. Cut through both layers around the rest of the circle.

3 Cut away stem on silk flower. Glue silk flower to front of card.

4 Trace and cut out half of a 4-inch circle from green card stock. Cut straight edge in

▶CONTINUED ON PAGE 102

Invitation
  Flower Invitation
Decorations
  Daisy Chain Necklace
  Flower Drinking Straws
  Stamped Floral Napkins & Tablecloth
Party Favors
  Painted Flowerpots
Activities
  Fun Flower Relay
  Pin the Flower on the Stem
  Flowerpot Toss
Food Fun
  Flower Sandwiches*
  Floral Crudités & Dip*
  Cheese & Fruit Tray*
  Iced Fruit Tea*
  Edible Flower Cupcakes*
  Frosted Butterfly or Flower Sugar Cookes*

Look for these recipes in the Food Fun chapter, pages 142–173. You'll find lots of EXTRA food ideas to choose from!

Flower Invitation

▶ CONTINUED FROM PAGE 101

the shape of a hill. Glue hill inside card.

5 Use pencil to write party activities for stems. Draw flowers, leaves and a butterfly inside invitation. Trace over pencil lines with marker. Print party information on hill.

6 Color in flowers and butterfly with pencil crayons.

7 *Option: Decorate envelope with flower rubber stamps.*

Daisy Chain Necklace

1 For each flower, bend one white chenille stem into five zigzags of the same size. Leave a little extra at the beginning and end.

2 Gently bring the ends together. Wrap an extra white stem through all the bends on the inside to hold the flower together.

3 Bend wire to round the bends on the outside to look like petals of a flower.

4 Glue a pompom in the center of each flower to cover any sharp ends.

5 Cut green chenille stem into 1-inch pieces. Connect daisies in a chain with green chenille pieces. The chain should be large enough to slip over a girl's head.

Things You'll Need

* 12–17 white chenille stems
* 2 green chenille stems
* 12–17 yellow ¼-inch pompoms
* Low-temperature glue gun and glue sticks
* Scissors

Other Ideas

• Decorate your table with small potted flowers. Print each guest's name on a flowerpot with markers. Place a pot by each place setting.

• Remove the heads from silk flowers. Scatter them across the tablecloth, or glue them in place.

• Put an edible flower in each section of an ice cube tray. Fill with water and freeze. Serve the ice cubes in your party drinks. They won't last long, but they are pretty!

• If you don't have blooming flowers in your own yard, use inexpensive silk flowers to decorate.

Flower Drinking Straws

1 For each straw, trace a small flower (page 181) onto craft foam. Cut out.

2 Cut two ½-inch slits next to each other in center of flower.

3 Thread straw through slits so that straw looks like the flower's stem.

4 Trace two small leaves onto green craft foam for each flower. Cut out. Trace a small flower center onto a contrasting color of craft foam.

5 Glue the center circle to flower over slits. Glue leaves behind flower.

Things You'll Need
* Green flexible drinking straws
* Scraps of craft foam in green and different colors
* Scissors
* Strong white glue
* Pencil
* Scissors

Stamped Floral Napkins & Tablecloth

Things You'll Need
* Plain white paper napkins
* Layered flower stamp*
* Acrylic craft paints
* Paintbrushes
*A Duncan Chunky Purple Posey stamp was used in this project.

1 Cover worktable. Open up napkins. Lay them out, all facing in the same direction.

2 *First layer:* Apply lighter shades of your chosen colors to the first stamp layer with paintbrushes. Work quickly.

3 Press stamp firmly to corner of each napkin.

4 Clean brushes and stamps before changing colors.

5 *Second layer:* Apply darker colors to second stamp layer with paintbrushes. Press firmly on top of first stamped images. Let dry.

6 Fold napkins.

7 Repeat steps 1–6 to decorate a paper or fabric tablecloth.

Painted Flowerpots

Paint the Flowerpot

Things You'll Need

For each flowerpot:
* Acrylic paints: blue, white, green and yellow
* Water-based outdoor sealer
* Paintbrushes
* Cotton swabs
* Alphabet rub-on transfers
* Wooden craft stick
* Small envelope (for seeds)
* Flower seeds
* Small rubber stamps with garden or flower theme (optional)
* Stamping ink pad (optional)
* Felt-tip markers
* Small self-sealing bag filled with soil or potting mix
* White or plain colored paper
* 8-inch piece of ⅛-inch ribbon
* Paper towels
* Ruler
* Scissors
* Pencil

*These products were used in this project: Plaid (Tulip) Letter Garden rub-on transfers; PSX Brushy Garden Pixie stamp set.

1 Paint body of flowerpot blue. Let dry. Repeat once or twice.

2 Paint the top rim of flowerpot green. Let dry. Repeat once or twice.

3 Paint a white oval in the center of the pot, over the blue. Let dry. Repeat.

4 Dip the end of a cotton swab into yellow paint. Dab off extra paint onto a paper towel. Press swab on edge of oval to make a dot. Repeat until there are dots all the way around the oval. Let dry.

5 Paint pot with sealer, inside and out. Let dry. Repeat two or three more times.

Transfers & Stamps

1 Cut out initials of your guests from sheet of rub-on transfers. Leave a border of at least ⅛ inch around each design.

2 Peel off backing sheet from rub-on. Lay rub-on over white oval. Press it in place with your fingers. Rub edge of craft stick over entire initial.

3 Slowly lift off clear film. If parts of design are not sticking, press film onto jar and rub again with craft stick.

Scroll

1 Using markers or pens, print "The Language of Flowers" information (page 105) on a sheet of paper. **Option**: *Print information using your computer.* Center and color the words.

2 Starting at the bottom, roll up the paper to make a tube. Tie ribbon in a bow around the tube. Cut ends at an angle.

3 Place bag of soil, seed envelopes and scroll in pot.

Fun Flower Relay

1 Divide guests into two teams. Line up half of one team on one side of the room and the other half on the other side. Repeat with other team.

2 Give the first player on each team a spoon. Place a flower on the spoon. (It will be harder to keep lightweight flowers on the spoons!)

3 Have the first player on each team hold the spoon in one hand and hold the other hand behind her back. The first players must race across the room and hand the spoon to a teammate without dropping the flower. If the flower falls, the player returns to the starting point.

4 Continue until all players have carried the flower. The first team to finish to finish is the winner.

Things You'll Need
* 2 spoons
* 2 silk flowers

The Language of Flowers

What do different flowers mean?

Anemones—Unfading love.
Buttercups—Cheerfulness.
Carnations (pink)—I'll never forget you.
Daffodils—Respect.
Forget-me-nots—True love, memories.
Gladiolas—Love at first sight.

Hydrangeas—Thank you for understanding.
Ivy—Friendship.
Lavender—Devotion.
Magnolias—Sweetness.
Orchids—Love, beauty.
Pansies—Thoughts, love.
Rose (pink)—Perfect happiness.
Rose (red)—I love you.

Rose (white)—Eternal love, innocence.
Rose (yellow)—Friendship.
Roses (white and red)—Unity.
Sweetpeas—Goodbye, thank you for a lovely time.
Tulips—Fame.
Zinnias—Thoughts of a friend.

Food Fun!

Set a blooming table with *Flower Sandwiches* and *Floral Crudités & Dip*. Your guests will buzz right over to sample the *Cheese & Fruit Tray*. Water them well with big glasses of *Iced Fruit Tea*. And don't forget dessert—*Edible Flower Cupcakes* and *Frosted Butterfly or Flower Sugar Cookes* are just the thing! Recipes and other fun ideas are found on pages 142–173.

Things You'll Need

* ★ Bright poster board
* ★ Jumbo green rickrack (or green craft foam or construction paper)
* ★ Silk or paper flowers
* ★ Tacks, pins, tape or poster putty
* ★ Craft glue
* ★ Masking tape
* ★ Colored felt-tip markers (optional)
* ★ Bandanna or scarf for blindfold
* ★ Prize

Pin the Flower on the Stem

Before Your Party

1 Glue green rickrack to poster board to make several flower stems.

2 Glue flower heads to all but two of the stems.

3 Color butterflies and ladybugs on the poster with markers, if you want.

When You're Ready to Play

1 Tack or tape poster to a wall, tree, door, etc.

2 Make two small rolls of masking tape, sticky side out. Press each one onto the back of a flower head.

3 Take turns, blindfolding each guest. Play "Pin the Tail on the Donkey," except see who can come closest to sticking the flower heads on the empty stems.

4 Award a small prize to the girl who comes closest.

Flowerpot Toss

Things You'll Need

* ★ 3 flowerpots
* ★ Ribbon, chalk or flower petals
* ★ 5 silk flowers
* ★ 5 quarters (optional)
* ★ Tape or hot-glue gun (optional)
* ★ Small prize

Let's Begin

1 Mark a throwing line using ribbon, chalk or flower petals.

2 Line up flowerpots 4–5 feet from throwing line. You can use pots of different sizes, if you want. Make the small ones worth more points. Or set up the pots at different heights.

3 Have each guest stand behind the throwing line. Then try to throw the flowers into the flowerpots. If the flowers are too lightweight to throw, tape or hot-glue a quarter to the back. If it is too easy, move the pots farther away.

4 Give a prize to the winner.

Holiday Parties

It's A New Year

Celebrate the holidays with your friends with these cool party themes!

New Year's Party

Celebrate the new year with your best friends. Play games, create a scrapbook and make memories. Complete the night by opening a surprise time capsule!

By Lorine Mason

Invitation
Pop-up Party Invitation

Decorations
Party Ware

Party Favors
New Year's Scrapbook

Activities
Time Capsule
"How Well Do You Know Me?" Game

Food Fun*
Faux Champagne*
Mini Pizza Bites*
Bagel Bites
Dogs in a Blanket*
Mini Brownie Cupcakes

*Look for these recipes in the Food Fun chapter, pages 142–173. You'll find lots of EXTRA food ideas to choose from!

Invitation

Pop-up Party Invitation

1 Cut a 4¾ x 6½-inch piece from green card stock. Cut a 4¼ x 6-inch piece of wrapping paper. Use the glue stick to glue the wrapping paper in the center of the card stock.

2 Cut a 3¾ x 5½-inch piece from pink card stock. Use the glue stick to glue it in the center of the wrapping paper.

3 Punch swirls from wrapping paper. Glue them to the front of the card.

4 Cut a 1⅜ x 7½-inch strip of green card stock. Use the black marker to print the party information across the strip. **Option:** *Use the computer to print the words on card stock, then cut strip.*

Things You'll Need

For each invitation:
* Foil wrapping paper
* Green and pink card stock (or 2 colors to match wrapping paper)
* White envelope
* Scissors
* Black fine-tip marker
* Paper punches: large and small swirls
* Glue stick
* Pencil
* Ruler
* Computer with printer (optional)

Invitation

5 Lay the strip print side up. Fold over the left end 1¼ inches. Keep folding the strip accordion-style, every 1¼ inches, until the whole strip is folded.

6 Cut two 1¾-inch squares from pink card stock. Cut two 2½-inch squares from green card stock. Glue the pink squares to the green squares. Glue the ends of the folded strip to the pink squares.

7 Glue the green square on the right end of the folded strip in the center of the card. Turn it at an angle.

8 Fold strip down. Glue a punched swirl to the green square at the other end of the folded strip.

9 Decorate the envelope flap with swirls punched from wrapping paper and card stock. Slide the invitation into the envelope, keeping the strip folded so it will "pop up" when the invitation is opened.

It's a New Year Party Sleepover and Scrapbooking Party
December 31st 8:00 p.m. - January 1st
Bring your sleeping bag, pillow, p.j.'s and photo's, ticket stubs, artwork or any other
memories that you would like to include in a Memories scrapbook.

Decorations

Party Ware

Champagne Glasses

Punch large swirls from foil wrapping paper. Coil them around the stems of plastic glasses.

Party Plates

Sprinkle confetti and swirls punched from wrapping paper on top of each paper plate. Cover each with a clear plastic plate.

Party Napkins

Punch swirls from napkins.

Another Idea: Party Table Cover

Choose a paper table cover to go with your decorations. Sprinkle it with swirls punched from wrapping paper and card stock. Scatter confetti over it.

Things You'll Need

★ Plastic champagne glasses
★ Paper napkins in desired color
★ Paper plates in desired color
★ Clear plastic plates the same size as paper plates
★ Foil wrapping paper
★ Card stock in colors to match wrapping paper
★ New Year's confetti
★ Paper punches: large and small swirls

New Year's Scrapbook

1 Measure the front of scrapbook. Use scissors to cut a piece of wrapping paper to cover it, as you like. You can cover the entire front cover or leave some of the cover showing. If you want to wrap it around the edges, allow ½–1 inch extra. *Note: Our scrapbook measures 10¾ x 12 inches. We cut the wrapping paper 9½ x 12 inches. We wrapped ½ inch around the side edge of the cover, and left 2 inches of the cover showing along the left edge.*

Things You'll Need

For each scrapbook:
* Wire-bound scrapbook
* Foil wrapping paper
* Card stock in colors to match wrapping paper
* Stickers
* Fine-tip markers: black, multi colors
* Paper punches, including a large swirl
* Glue stick
* Scissors
* Pencil
* Eraser
* Ruler
* Computer with printer (optional)

2 Cover the scrapbook with glue where the paper will be placed. Lay paper on top. Smooth out any bubbles with your fingers. Put glue on the edges of the paper. Wrap them around to the inside of the cover.

3 Use a marker to write, "It's A New Year Memories by" on card stock. Glue it onto the cover. *Option: Use a computer to print the words on card stock.*

4 Use the large swirl punch to make shapes from extra wrapping paper. Glue them to card stock, overlapping some pieces.

5 Decorate your scrapbook as you wish with colorful paper, card stock and stickers. Use scissors, decorative paper edgers and other scrapbooking supplies.

It's A New Year Memories by

Time Capsule

Before Your Party

1 Ask an adult to help you cut the top off the bottle, leaving a 5-inch-tall piece. Wrap wrapping paper around the bottle. Use a glue stick to glue paper to bottle. Fold extra paper over the top edge.

2 Cut a piece of card stock 8 x 3½ inches. Use a marker to write "It's A New Year Time Capsule" and "Do Not Open before 12:00 a.m." on card stock. Glue it around bottle. *Option: Use a computer to print the words on card stock.*

3 Punch a few swirls from extra wrapping paper. Trim little pieces from the foam squares to fit on back of the swirls. Stick the swirls onto the bottle, overlapping the edges of the label.

4 Set the bottle open end down on card stock. Trace around bottle twice with a pencil. Cut out circles with scissors. Glue a swirl punched from wrapping paper in the center of each circle.

5 Fill the bottle with prizes and favors. Glue one card stock circle on the bottom of the bottle. Glue the other over the open end.

At Your Party

Ask an adult to remind you when it is a few minutes before midnight. Count down the last seconds before 12 o'clock. Let everyone break into his or her time capsule to celebrate the New Year!

Things You'll Need

For each time capsule:

* Recyclable 20-ounce plastic soda bottle (A straight bottle will work better than a curvy one.)
* Foil wrapping paper
* Card stock in colors to match wrapping paper
* Black fine-tip marker
* Paper punches: large and small swirls
* Favors to fill each bottle: candy, bottle of bubbles, tiny bottle of sparkling cider with your own label, small date book or pocket calendar, New Year's socks, etc.
* Glue stick
* Scissors
* Pencil
* Eraser
* Ruler
* Computer with printer (optional)

It's A New Ye
Time Capsule
Do Not Open before
12:00 a.m.

"How Well Do You Know Me?" Game

Before Your Party

 Cut six 4¼ x 3¼-inch game cards *for each player* from card stock.

 Using the marker, write a clue at the top of each card:

"What is my favorite pet?"
"What is something you might not know about me?"
"What is something I refuse to eat?"
"What is something I love to eat?"
"How many brothers do I have?"
"How many sisters do I have?"
"What is my favorite color?"

After each question, provide three spaces, numbered 1, 2 and 3, for answers.

3 Repeat to make a set of identical cards for each player. **Option:** *Print the cards using a computer.*

At Your Party

1 Give each guest a set of cards and a pencil. Give them a few minutes to write one true answer and two false answers on each card.

 Let guests take turns reading one card with the question and all three answers. The first guest to guess which answer is correct gets to keep that card.

 Keep taking turns until each guest has had a chance to read each of her cards. The person holding the most cards at the end of the game wins.

Food Fun!

Toast the New Year with *Faux Champagne* and enjoy nibbling on your favorite finger foods—*Mini Pizza Bites and Dogs in Blankets.* Recipes and serving ideas can be found on pages 142–173.

Things You'll Need

* Card stock in different colors
* Scissors
* Paper trimmer (optional)
* Black fine-tip marker
* Computer with printer (optional)
* Pencil for each guest

Valentine's Day Party

Valentine's Day is a time to share friendship. This party is Cupid-approved and straight from the heart.

By Mary Ayres

Invitation

"Toadally Yours"

Things You'll Need

For each invitation:
* 8½ x 11-inch card stock: white, pink, red
* White paper
* Black markers: fine-tip, bullet-tip
* Red fine-tip marker
* paper punches: heart and ¼-inch circle
* Decorative-edge scissors: caterpillar
* Scissors
* Paper glue
* Pencil
* Eraser
* Ruler
* Computer with color printer (optional)

1 Cut a 5½ x 8½-inch piece from pink card stock. Fold in half to make a 4¼ x 5½-inch card.

2 Use a pencil to trace toad's outline and face (page 186) onto white paper.

3 Turn paper over. Trace over the lines you traced in step 2.

4 Turn the pattern right side up. Lay it on top of the card. Trace over the toad outlines and face again with a pencil. The lines will now be on the invitation. Cut out toad along dashed lines.

5 Punch two hearts from red paper. Glue hearts to ends of mouth.

6 Use black bullet-tip marker to draw eyes. Use black fine-tip marker to draw nostrils, mouth and a line around toad, close to edge.

▶ CONTINUED ON PAGE 114

Invitation
  "Toadally Yours"
Decorations
  Valentine Puppy Pouch
Party Favors
  Kitty Candy Bag
Activities
  Drop the Lovebugs in the Jar
Food Fun
  Monkey Cupcakes*

*Look for this recipe in the Food Fun chapter, pages 142–173. You'll find lots of EXTRA food ideas to choose from!

you're invited to a "toadally" fun Valentine party

Invitation

▶ CONTINUED FROM PAGE 113

7 Use pencil to trace tummy (page 186) onto white paper. Cut out. Trace and cut tummy from white card stock. Trim curved edges with caterpillar scissors.

8 Use red fine-tip marker to write words in center of tummy. *Option: Use computer and printer to print words in red ink on white paper. Trace and cut out tummy shape around lettering.*

9 Use black fine-tip marker to draw a line around tummy, close to edge.

10 Punch a heart from red card stock. Glue to center top of tummy. Glue tummy to toad.

11 Punch 12¼-inch circles from white paper. Glue around face and beside tummy. See dots on pattern.

12 Write party information inside card using fine-tip black or red marker.

♥

you're invited to a "toadally" fun Valentine party

Decorations

Valentine Puppy Pouch

Make the Head

1 Cover worktable with tablecloth or plastic bags.

2 Using snake scissors, cut 2 inches off one side of two 9-inch paper plates.

3 Paint back sides of plates pink. For nose, paint one side and edges of wooden heart red. Let dry.

Face

1 Use pencil to trace the puppy face (page 187) onto white paper.

2 Turn paper over. Trace over the lines you traced in step 1.

3 Turn the pattern right side up. Lay it on the pink side of one paper plate with cut edge at top. Trace over the pattern lines again with a pencil. The lines will now be on the paper plate.

Things You'll Need

For each pouch:
* Waterproof tablecloth or plastic trash bags
* Red card stock
* White paper
* Paper plates: 2 (9-inch), 1 (7-inch)
* Black metallic cord
* 2-inch wooden heart
* 2 (⅞-inch) flat black buttons
* Paints: white, pink, red
* Paintbrush
* Paper towels
* Black bullet-tip marker
* Paper punches: heart, ⅛-inch circle
* Decorative-edge scissors: snake
* Scissors
* Paper glue
* Craft glue
* Pencil
* Eraser
* Ruler

For cheeks, dip a dry paintbrush in red paint. Wipe most of the paint off on a paper towel. Swirl brush in a circle on puppy's cheeks.

 Paint the eye circle white. For cheek dots, dip the tip of paintbrush handle into white paint. Make a small dot in each cheek. Let dry.

6 Use the black bullet-tip marker to draw the mouth, freckles, and a line around the eye circle. Draw a line around the red nose, close to the edge.

Put It Together

1 Hold plates together with pink sides facing outward. Use the ⅛-inch circle punch to make a line of holes around curved edges, 1 inch apart and ¼ inch from edge.

2 Thread the cord through the top pair of holes on one side. Tie cord in a knot around the edges of the plates, leaving a 10-inch tail.

3 "Sew" plates together with cord, wrapping the cord around the edges of plates. Knot the cord again in the last two holes.

4 Trim the end of the cord, leaving a 10-inch tail. For hanger, knot the cord ends together.

Finishing Touches

1 Use craft glue to glue button eyes and red heart nose to puppy's face.

2 For ears, use the snake scissors to cut the 7-inch plate in half. Turn pieces over so backs are facing you. Using the black bullet-tip marker, draw an outline around the ears, close to the edge.

3 Punch hearts from red card stock. Use the paper glue to glue them all over the ears. Point them in different directions.

4 Glue the ears to the top corners of the pouch. Let dry.

5 Place valentines in pouch.

Kitty Candy Bag

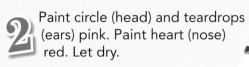

Kitty Candy Bag

Things You'll Need

For each bag:

* ✶ Waterproof tablecloth or plastic trash bags
* ✶ 12 inches of ⅝-inch pink-and-gingham ribbon
* ✶ Wooden cutout shapes: 1 (2½-inch) circle, 2 (2-inch) teardrops, 1 (¾-inch) heart
* ✶ Scrap of pink felt
* ✶ Paints: white, pink, red
* ✶ Paintbrush
* ✶ Plastic zippered sandwich bag
* ✶ Candies
* ✶ Red and black markers: fine-tip, bullet-tip
* ✶ Cellophane tape
* ✶ Craft glue
* ✶ Scissors
* ✶ Pencil
* ✶ Eraser
* ✶ Ruler

Painting

1 Cover worktable with tablecloth or plastic bags.

2 Paint circle (head) and teardrops (ears) pink. Paint heart (nose) red. Let dry.

Kitty's Head

1 Using a pencil, trace details for kitty's face (page 186) onto white paper.

2 Turn paper over. Trace over the lines you traced in step 1.

3 Turn the pattern right side up. Lay it on pink circle. Trace over the pattern lines with a pencil. The lines will now be on the pink circle.

4 For cheeks, dip a dry paintbrush in red paint. Wipe most of the paint off on a paper towel. Swirl the brush in a circle on kitty's cheeks.

5 For cheek dots, dip the tip of paintbrush handle into white paint. Make a small dot in each cheek. Let dry.

6 Use the red bullet-tip marker to draw stripes on sides and top of head. Use the black bullet-tip marker to draw eyes. Use the black fine-tip marker to draw mouth and freckles. Draw outlines around head, ears and the red nose, close to the edge.

7 Glue ears to back of head. Glue nose to face.

8 Tie ribbon in a bow. Cut ends in a "V." Glue bow to bottom of kitty's head.

Put It Together

1 Make tiny folds along the bottom of the sandwich bag. Place tape on folds to hold them.

2 Glue folds to back of kitty's head. Cut a 2¼-inch circle of pink felt. Glue it to back of head, over folds. Let dry.

3 Fill bag with candy. Close bag.

Drop the Lovebugs in the Jar

Make Lovebugs

 To make love bugs, paint clothespins pink. Let dry.

 For eyes, use black fine-tip marker to make two dots near top of head.

 For antennae, wrap a pipe cleaner around the neck of the clothespin. Twist ends together in back. Bend ends up over the head and shape into antennae.

 Punch a heart from red card stock. Glue it to the center of bug's body.

 Repeat steps 1–4 to make a total of four lovebugs.

Decorate the Jar

 Trace heart pattern (page 186) onto white paper. Cut out. Trace and cut out heart from red card stock.

 Use black bullet-tip marker to write "hugs inside" on heart.

 Glue heart to pink card stock. Cut around edge of heart with caterpillar scissors, leaving a pink border.

 Punch two ¼-inch holes in sides of heart at circles on pattern.

 Cut cord in half. Fold one piece in half. Thread both cut ends through one hole from back to front. Bring cut ends through loop formed by cord. Tighten loop gently. Repeat with other cord in other hole.

 Glue heart to jar. Tie ends of cord in a bow on back of jar. Trim ends even.

 Wrap and glue ribbon around top of jar with craft glue. Tie ribbon in a bow on front of jar. Cut ends in a "V."

To play: *Have guests take turns standing over jar. See who can drop the most lovebugs into the jar.*

Things You'll Need

* 8½ x 11-inch card stock: pink, red
* 54 inches black metallic cord
* 18 inches of ⅝-inch pink-and-white gingham ribbon
* 4 wooden doll clothespins
* 4 white 6-inch chenille stems
* Quart jar
* Craft glue
* Decorative-edge scissors: caterpillar
* Scissors
* Black markers: fine-tip, bullet-tip
* Paper punches: heart, ¼-inch circle
* Pencil
* Eraser
* Ruler

 Food Fun! Who wouldn't love *Monkey Cupcakes*? Find these and other loveable food ideas beginning on page 142.

Bunny Party

Every bunny loves to have fun at Easter! Check out these cool projects and fun ideas!

By Mary Ayres

Invitation
Bunny Invitation
Decorations
Bunny Shakers
Party Favors
Bunny Bags
Activities
Pin the Nose on the Bunny
Food Fun
Bunny Cupcakes*

Look for this recipe in the Food Fun chapter, pages 142–173. You'll find lots of EXTRA food ideas to choose from!

Invitation

Bunny Invitation

1 Trace bunny card and bow patterns (page 188) onto white paper. Cut out. Trace and cut bunny card from white card stock. Fold ears down (dashed lines on pattern).

2 Use black fine-tip marker to draw "blanket stitches" around cut edges of ears.

3 Use a pencil to trace bunny's eyes, nose and mouth onto white paper.

4 Turn paper over. Trace over the lines you traced in step 3.

5 Turn the pattern right side up again. Lay it on top of the card. Trace over the face again with a pencil. The lines will now be on the invitation.

6 Paint nose baby pink. Let dry.

Things You'll Need
For each invitation:
* 8½ x 11-inch card stock: white, bright purple, green
* White paper
* Baby pink paint
* Paintbrush
* Paper towels
* Black fine-tip marker
* ¼-inch circle paper punch
* Paper glue
* Scissors
* Pencil
* Eraser
* Ruler

7 For cheeks, dip a paintbrush in baby pink paint. Wipe most of the paint off on a paper towel. Swirl the brush in a circle on bunny's cheeks. Let dry.

8 Go over pencil lines with fine-tip marker. Draw solid lines for eyes. Draw dashed lines for nose and mouth. Let dry. Erase pencil lines.

9 Trace and cut bow from purple card stock. Use fine-tip marker to draw "blanket stitches" around edges.

10 Punch seven circles from green card stock. Glue them to bow tie with paper glue. Glue bow tie to card.

11 Use fine-tip marker to print party information under bunny's ears.

Food Fun! Guests will come hopping up for fun *Bunny Cupcakes.* Look for this and other fun food ideas on pages 142–173.

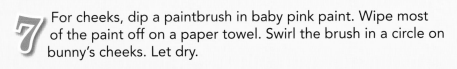

Things You'll Need

For each shaker:
* Waterproof tablecloth or plastic trash bags
* 8½ x 11-inch card stock: green, blue
* 3 (6-inch) paper plates
* Handful of dry beans
* White paper
* Jumbo craft stick
* 1-inch pink pompom
* Baby pink paint
* Paintbrush
* Paper towels
* Stapler with staples
* Black fine-tip marker
* ⁹⁄₁₆-inch circle paper punch
* Paper glue
* Craft glue
* Scissors
* Pencil
* Eraser
* Ruler

Decorations

Bunny Shakers

1 Cover worktable with tablecloth or plastic bags.

2 Use a pencil to trace pattern for large bunny face (page 189) onto white paper.

3 Turn paper over. Trace over the lines you traced in step 2.

4 Turn the pattern right side up again. Lay it on the wrong side of a 6-inch paper plate. Trace over the lines again with a pencil. The lines will now be on the paper plate.

5 For ears, cut a second 6-inch paper plate in half.

▶ CONTINUED ON PAGE 121

Pin the Nose on the Bunny

Make the Background

1 Cover worktable with tablecloth or plastic bags.

2 Cut a 12 x 20-inch piece from blue sky poster board.

3 For grass, cut a 2½ x 12-inch piece from green printed paper. For top of grass, cut along one long edge with wide pinking scissors. Glue grass to bottom of poster board.

Make the Bunny

1 Use a pencil to trace bunny's eyes and mouth lines from pattern for large bunny face (page 189) onto white paper.

2 Turn paper over. Trace over the lines you traced in step 2.

3 Turn the pattern right side up again. Lay it on the wrong side of a 6-inch paper plate. Trace over the lines again with a pencil. The lines will now be on the paper plate.

4 For ears, cut a second 6-inch paper plate in half.

5 For cheeks, dip a paintbrush in baby pink paint. Wipe most of the paint off on a paper towel. Swirl the brush in a circle on bunny's cheeks, and down centers of ears. Let dry.

6 Go over lines of face with black fine-tip marker. Draw solid lines for eyes. Draw dashed lines for nose and mouth. Let dry. Erase any pencil lines

7 Glue ears behind top of head. Crumple a paper towel and place it behind head. Glue edges of head and ears to center of background, near top.

8 Place crumpled paper towels behind the 9-inch paper plate and glue edges to background, overlapping bottom of head. For tail, glue white pompom to right side of plate.

9 Trace bow loops and bow center patterns (page 189) onto white paper. Trace and cut two bow loops and one center from bright pink paper.

10 Use the black fine-tip marker to draw "blanket stitches" around the edges of each piece.

11 Glue the points of the bow loops to

Things You'll Need

* Waterproof tablecloth or plastic trash bags
* 8½ x 11-inch card stock: pink, orange
* Paper plates: 1 (9-inch), 2 (6-inch)
* Blue sky poster board
* 12-inch square green print paper
* White paper
* Pompoms: 1-inch pink, 1½-inch white
* Baby pink paint
* Paintbrush
* Paper towels
* Decorative-edge scissors: wide pinking
* Black fine-tip marker
* ⁹⁄₁₆-inch circle paper punch
* Double-stick tape
* Poster putty
* Craft glue
* Scissors
* Pencil
* Eraser
* Ruler

the back of bow center with paper glue.

 Punch 13 circles from orange paper. Glue them to bow with paper glue.

 Glue bow to bunny's neck.

Game Pieces

1 For noses, punch 9⁄16-inch circles from assorted colors of paper. Use black fine-tip marker to draw "blanket stitches" around edges and print numbers (1 through 10) in center.

2 Glue a paper circle to each pompom. Press a piece of double-stick tape to opposite side of pompom so that noses will stick.

To play: *Put up the bunny on a door or wall with poster putty or tacks. Blindfold guests one at a time and let them try to stick a pompom nose on the bunny. Give a prize to the one who comes closest to getting it in the right place.*

Decorations

▶CONTINUED FROM PAGE 119

6 For cheeks, dip a paintbrush in baby pink paint. Wipe most of the paint off on a paper towel. Swirl the brush in a circle on bunny's cheeks, and down centers of ears. Let dry.

7 Go over pencil lines of face with fine-tip marker. Draw solid lines for eyes. Draw dashed lines for nose and mouth. Let dry. Erase pencil lines.

8 For nose, glue a pink pompom to center top of mouth.

9 Glue ears behind top of head. Glue jumbo craft stick to back of head at center bottom.

10 Place a handful of beans in remaining paper plate for back of head. Glue head plates together along outside edges. Sandwich the ends of the ears and the tip of the craft stick in between. Let dry, then staple the edges together.

11 Trace patterns for bow loop and bow center (page 189) onto white paper. Cut out. Trace and cut two bow loops and one center from blue paper.

12 Use the fine-tip marker to draw "blanket stitches" around the edges of each piece.

13 Glue the points of the bow loops to the back of bow center with paper glue.

14 Punch 13 small circles from green paper. Glue them to bow with paper glue.

15 Glue bow to bottom of head.

Bunny Bags

1 Cover worktable with tablecloth or plastic bags.

2 Paint the 2½-inch circle (head) and ovals (ears) white. Paint the ¾-inch circle (bow-tie knot) and hearts (bow loops) olive green. Let dry.

Face & Details

1 Use a pencil to trace the bunny's eyes, nose and mouth from the bunny bag pattern (page 189) onto white paper.

2 Turn paper over. Trace over the lines you traced in step 1.

3 Turn the pattern right side up again. Lay it on the white head. Trace over the pattern lines again with a pencil. The lines will now be on the white circle.

4 For cheeks, dip a paintbrush in bright pink paint. Wipe most of the paint off on a paper towel. Swirl the brush in a circle on bunny's cheeks, and down centers of ears.

5 Paint nose baby pink.

6 To paint the dots on bow tie, dip the tip of your paintbrush

handle into bright blue paint. Make small dots all over the tie. Let dry.

7 Use the fine-tip marker to draw solid lines for eyes and dashed lines for mouth and nose.

8 Use the fine-tip marker to draw "blanket stitch" around edges of head, ears and pieces for bow tie.

Put Bunny Together

1 For the bow tie, glue the points of the hearts behind the olive green circle. Glue the bow tie to bottom of head.

2 Glue ears to the side of the head.

Put Bag Together

1 Trim top of bag with cloud scissors. Use bullet-tip marker to print guest's name on bottom front of bag.

2 Fold top of bag over 2¾ inches to front. Measure down 2¼ inches from fold and 1¾ inches in from left side. Mark spot with a pencil. Mark another spot 2¼ inches down from fold and 1¾ inches in from right side. Punch holes through all layers at spots.

3 Fill bag with goodies. Fold top of bag over onto front.

4 Stick pieces of magnetic tape on back of bunny. Bunny can be used as a refrigerator magnet after the party.

5 Thread ends of cord through holes from back to front. Tie ends in a bow, tying cord around bunny's head. Trim cord ends.

Things You'll Need

For each bag:
* Waterproof tablecloth or plastic trash bags
* 6 x 3⅝ x 11-inch pink paper bag
* Wooden cutout shapes: 1 (¾-inch) circle, 1 (2½-inch) circle, 2 (2⅝-inch) ovals, 2 (1½-inch) hearts
* Paints: white, baby pink, bright pink, olive green, bright blue
* White paper
* White cord
* Paintbrush
* Paper towels
* Decorative-edge scissors: cloud
* Scissors
* Black markers: bullet-tip, fine-tip
* ¼-inch circle paper punch
* 2 (1½-inch) pieces magnetic tape
* Craft glue
* Pencil
* Eraser
* Ruler

Candy-Corny Costume Party

Dress up to celebrate the fun of the fall season. Pick a special theme (like scarecrows or candy) or wear fall colors of yellow, gold, red and orange.

By Sandy Rollinger

Invitation

Candy-Corny Invitation

Measuring & Cutting

1 Cover worktable with tablecloth or plastic bags.

2 Trace patterns for invitation candy corn, pumpkin, and pumpkin stem (page 190) onto white paper. Cut out.

3 Trace and cut candy corn from white card stock, yellow paper and orange paper. Cut pumpkin from orange paper, and stem from green paper. Erase any pencil lines. *Option: Use computer to print words on orange paper. Cut pumpkin shape around words.*

4 Cut the top part off the yellow candy corn. Glue to white candy corn with glue stick, matching edges.

5 Cut the top two parts off the orange candy corn. Glue to yellow candy corn with glue stick, matching edges.

▶CONTINUED ON PAGE 124

Invitation
  Candy-Corny Invitation
Decorations
  Pumpkin & Corn Bowl
  Pumpkin Chest
  Pumpkin & Corn
    Garland
Party Favors
  Fall Bead Necklaces
  Candy Cups
Activities
  Corny Games
Food Fun
  Twinkie Centipedes*
  Pumpkin Pudding
    Treats*

*Look for these recipes in the Food Fun chapter, pages 142–173. You'll find lots of EXTRA food ideas to choose from!

PLACE
DATE
TIME
PHONE
PRIZES FOR THE FUNNIEST, SCARIEST, AND THE PRETTIEST COSTUME!

▶ CONTINUED FROM PAGE 123

Things You'll Need

For each invitation:

* Waterproof tablecloth or plastic trash bags
* 3 x 5-inch white invitation card with envelope
* Plain or small-print paper: orange, yellow, green, lavender
* White card stock
* 2 (7mm) wiggly eyes
* 9 inches of ¼-inch purple satin ribbon
* ½-inch wooden plug
* Paints: red, black, white
* Paintbrush
* Nail or pointed scissors
* Yellow metal eyelet
* Eyelet-setting tool
* Small hammer
* Wood block
* Paper plate
* Black ultra-fine-tip marker
* Paper punches: spiral, ⅛-inch circle
* Decorative-edge scissors: ripple
* Scissors
* Double-stick tape
* Glue stick
* Craft glue
* Toothpick
* Pencil
* Eraser
* Ruler
* Computer with printer (optional)

6 Use marker to draw outline of squiggles and dots around outside edge and between candy corn parts.

7 Measure and cut 2¾ x 4¾-inch rectangle from lavender paper. Trim edges with ripple scissors. Glue to front of card with glue stick.

Put It Together

1 Measure down 1 inch from top edge of card and 3 inches in from right edge. Mark a small dot with pencil.

2 Ask an adult to help with the eyelet. Make a small hole at the dot using a nail or tip of sharp scissors. Make another hole near top of candy corn (shown as a dot on pattern).

3 Push eyelet through hole in candy corn, then invitation. Fit eyelet end on back. Place on a wood block. Set tip of eyelet tool in eyelet. Gently tap the tool with a hammer to fasten eyelet.

4 Use marker to print "BOO! You are invited to a Halloween Costume Party" on yellow paper. Cut candy corn shape around words, slightly smaller than candy corn on card. *Option: Use computer to print words on yellow paper. Cut candy-corn shape around words.*

5 Glue yellow shape onto front of card underneath candy corn.

Food Fun! Your guests will love *Twinkie Centipedes* and *Pumpkin Pudding Treats!* Look on pages 142-173 for these recipes and other yummy, fun ideas.

Pumpkins & Candy Corn

Pumpkin

1 Trace patterns for pumpkin and large pumpkin stem (page 190) onto white paper. Use a pencil to trace pumpkin onto orange foam and stem onto green foam.

2 Mix a little yellow and pumpkin paint on paper plate. Dip sponge into paint. Dab it lightly over pumpkin. Do not cover the foam completely.

3 Clean sponge in water. Squeeze out water. Mix a little yellow and green paint on paper plate. Dip sponge into paint. Dab it lightly over green stem.

4 Let paints dry for 1 hour. Cut out pumpkin and stem along pencil lines.

5 Use marker to draw outline of squiggles and dots around edge of pumpkin and stem.

6 Press a small piece of double-stick tape onto the paper plate. For nose, stick wooden plug on tape. Paint plug bright red. Let dry.

7 Use toothpick to put glue on back of wiggly eyes and nose. Glue to pumpkin.

8 Draw squiggly smile and eyebrows with black paint. Paint a small "comma" for white highlight on nose. Let dry.

9 Tie ribbon in a bow. Cut ends at a slant. Glue bow to center bottom of pumpkin.

10 Dip cotton swab in pink blush. Dab onto cheeks. Glue green stem to top of pumpkin.

Candy Corn

1 Trace pattern for candy corn (page 190) onto white paper. Use a pencil to trace candy corn onto yellow craft foam.

2 Squeeze puddles of white, yellow, red and pumpkin paints onto paper plate.

3 Dip sponge into white paint. Dab it lightly on top third of candy corn. Do not cover the foam completely.

4 Clean sponge in water. Squeeze out water. Dip sponge in yellow paint. Dab paint lightly across center of candy corn.

5 Clean sponge in water. Squeeze out water. Dip sponge in pumpkin paint. Dab lightly across bottom third of candy corn. Let dry for 1 hour.

6 Cut out along pencil line. Use marker to draw outline of squiggles and dots around edge and between stripes.

7 Finish by following steps 6–10 for pumpkin, omitting stem.

Pumpkin & Corn Bowl

Things You'll Need

* ✶ Waterproof tablecloth or plastic trash bags
* ✶ 6 Pumpkins (see page 125)
* ✶ 6 Candy Corns (see page 125)
* ✶ 4-inch-deep, 10-inch-diameter bright green plastic bowl
* ✶ 5½-inch-tall bright green plastic drinking glass
* ✶ Purple jumbo rickrack
* ✶ Quick-setting glue
* ✶ Craft glue
* ✶ Scissors
* ✶ Toothpick
* ✶ Ruler

1 Turn glass upside down. Glue in center of bowl with quick-setting glue. Let dry overnight.

2 Glue rickrack around top and bottom of bowl with craft glue. Let dry.

3 Glue four pumpkins and four candy corns around bowl with craft glue, alternating them. They should stick up ¾ inch above edge.

4 Glue two pumpkins and two candy corns around top of drinking glass with craft glue, alternating them. They should stick up 2½ inches above edge.

5 Let glue dry for at least 2 hours. Fill bowl with popcorn, pretzels or other snacks.

Pumpkin Chest

Painting

1 Cover worktable with tablecloth or plastic bags.

2 Trace pattern for pumpkin chest leaf (page 190) onto white paper. Use a pencil to trace pattern five times onto green foam.

3 Mix a little yellow and bright green paint on paper plate. Dip sponge in paint. Dab it lightly over leaves. Do not cover the foam completely.

4 Let paints dry for 1 hour. Cut out leaves along pencil lines.

5 Use marker to draw squiggles and dots around edges of leaves.

Things You'll Need

* ✶ Waterproof tablecloth or plastic trash bags
* ✶ 2 (6-inch) round plastic bowls: orange, yellow or white
* ✶ Craft foam: green, orange
* ✶ White paper
* ✶ 8-inch green chenille stem
* ✶ 2 (7mm) wiggly eyes
* ✶ ½-inch wooden plug
* ✶ 1½ yards (¼-inch) purple satin ribbon
* ✶ Paint for plastic*: pumpkin, yellow, bright green, red
* ✶ Paint for paper*: white, black
* ✶ Small paintbrush
* ✶ 1-inch pieces cut from a clean kitchen sponge
* ✶ Paper plate
* ✶ Container of water
* ✶ Paper towels
* ✶ Toothpick
* ✶ Black fine-tip marker
* ✶ Double-stick tape
* ✶ Craft glue
* ✶ Scissors
* ✶ Pencil
* ✶ Ruler

*Plaid Enterprises provided the paints for plastic and paper used on these projects.

6 Mix a little pumpkin and yellow paint on paper plate. Dip sponge in paint. Dab it over outside of bowls. Let dry.

7 Press a small piece of double-stick tape onto the paper plate. For nose, stick wooden plug on tape. Paint plug red. Let dry.

Put It Together

1 Turn one bowl upside-down on top of the other. To make a hinge, cut a ½ x 2-inch strip of orange foam. Glue half of strip to top bowl and half of strip to bottom bowl. Turn bowls so hinge is in back.

2 Glue leaves on top of bowl so points meet in the center.

3 Wrap the chenille stem around a pencil to make a coil. Slide coil off. Glue one end to center of leaves.

4 Glue eyes and nose to top bowl. Draw a squiggly smile and eyebrows with black paint. Paint white highlight on nose. Let dry.

5 Tie ribbon in a bow. Glue to center bottom of bowl.

6 Fill bowl with snacks, treats or favors.

Pumpkin & Corn Garland

1 Cut a 10 x ½-inch strip of orange craft foam. Lay flat on your worktable.

2 Cut six 8-inch pieces of each color of ribbon: purple, orange, and yellow. Glue one end of each ribbon to craft foam strip, alternating colors. Leave about ¹⁄₁₆ inch space between ribbons.

3 Cut strip into sections, cutting after every sixth ribbon. Glue a section to the back of each candy corn and pumpkin so ribbons dangle down. Let dry.

4 Lay rickrack out flat. Place top of pumpkins and candy corn on rickrack, 4 inches apart. Glue in place. Let dry.

5 Put poster putty on ends of rickrack. Hang on a wall or over a doorway.

Things You'll Need

* 4 Pumpkins (see page 125)
* 4 Candy Corns (see page 125)
* Orange craft foam
* 1 yard purple medium rickrack
* 1⅓ yards (each color) of ⅛-inch satin ribbon: purple, orange, yellow
* Poster putty
* Craft glue
* Toothpick
* Scissors
* Ruler

Fall Bead Necklaces

Pumpkins & Candy Corn

1 Trace patterns for the small pumpkin, small pumpkin stem and small candy corn (page 190 and 191) onto white paper.

2 Make a small pumpkin or candy corn following the general instructions for Pumpkins & Candy Corn (page 125). Use the smaller eyes and wooden plugs listed in the materials list at right.

3 Fold orange ribbon in half to find center.

4 Spread glue on back of tab at top of pumpkin or candy corn. Fold tab over center of ribbon and press onto back of craft foam. Hold tab with a small, spring-type clothespin until glue dries.

5 Glue stem to front of pumpkin.

6 String eight pony beads on each side of necklace, alternating colors.

7 Tie ends of ribbon together in a knot.

Candy Cups

Things You'll Need

For each cup:
* Pumpkin or Candy Corn (see page 125)
* Paper nut/candy cup
* Craft glue
* Nuts or candies

Glue a finished Pumpkin or Candy Corn to the front of each nut cup. Pinch sides of cup with your fingers if needed so cups will stand up. Fill with nuts or candies.

Things You'll Need

Each necklace:
* 24 inches of ⅛-inch orange satin ribbon
* 6 inches of ¼-inch purple satin ribbon
* Pony beads: 6 yellow, 6 white, 4 orange
* Paint for paper*: white, black
* Small paintbrush
* 1-inch pieces cut from a clean kitchen sponge
* Cotton swabs
* Pink blush or chalk
* Paper plate
* White paper
* Container of water
* Paper towels
* Small spring-type clothespin
* Black fine-tip marker
* Double-stick tape
* Craft glue
* Scissors
* Toothpick
* Pencil
* Ruler

Each pumpkin necklace:
* Craft foam: orange, green
* Paints for plastic*: pumpkin, bright green, red
* ¼-inch wooden plug
* 2 (6mm) wiggly eyes

Each candy-corn necklace:
* Craft foam: yellow or white
* Paints for plastic*: white, yellow, pumpkin, red
* ¼-inch wooden plug
* 2 (6mm) wiggly eyes

*Plaid Enterprises provided the paints for plastic and paper used for these projects.

Corny Games

Set the Mood

Play a CD or tape of silly songs or sound effects during your party.

Take turns telling some funny jokes.

Ask your guests to share the funniest thing that ever happened to them.

Memory Game

Have everyone sit in a circle. Ask one person to start by naming his or her favorite funny character—from a cartoon, movie, or book. The next person in the circle names that one *and* her favorite silly character.

Go on around the circle, taking turns repeating the list and adding to it. (Ask an adult to help out by keeping the list with pencil and paper.) Anyone who repeats a character, misses one or gets them in the wrong order is out.

The last person left is the winner.

Costume Contest

Have everyone vote for his or her favorite costumes—funniest, most colorful, most unusual, etc. Give a prize to each winner.

Surprise Prizes

Before your party, wrap several small prizes in brown, orange and yellow paper. Place them in a bowl, bag or basket.

Let each winner of a game choose a prize, but don't open them until everyone has one. Then open them together.

Secret Santa Party

It's sure to be a merry Christmas when you gather with your friends for food, fun and festivities! You'll have a great time trying to figure out who your Secret Santa is! Ho! Ho! Ho!

By Sandy Rollinger

Invitation

Invitation
Secret Santa Party Invitation

Decorations
Santa Snowflakes
Sparkling Snowflakes
Santa Party Cups
Santa Light Garland

Party Favors
Santa Party Favor Bags

Activities
Name That Holiday Tune
Blindfolded Art
"Twas the Night Before Christmas …"
Surprise Favors & Prizes
Santa Gift Exchange

Food Fun
Santa Face Cake*

Look for this recipe in the Food Fun chapter, pages 142–173. You'll find lots of EXTRA food ideas to choose from!

PARTY DATE................
TIME..................
PLACE.................
PHONE................
PLEASE BRING A $.......... WRAPPED
EXCHANGE GIFT WITH YOUR NAME
ON THE INSIDE ONLY.

Secret Santa Party Invitation

Cut It Out

 Cover worktable with tablecloth or plastic bags.

 Trace patterns for suit, gift box, beard, hat trim, suit trim, face and mittens (page 192) on white paper. Cut out.

 Trace and cut from card stock: suit from red, gift box from green, face from pink and two mittens from blue.

4 Run white card stock through paper crimper. Trace around beard, hat trim and suit trim on crimped card stock. Cut out.

5 For background, measure and cut a 2¾ x 4½-inch rectangle from polka-dot paper.

6 Erase pencil lines from all pieces.

Put It Together

1 Glue polka-dot piece to center of card. Glue suit onto polka-dot paper.

2 Glue face onto beard, matching top edges. Glue beard onto suit.

3 Glue suit trim along bottom of suit. Glue hat trim to hat, covering edges of face and beard.

4 Use fine-tip marker to print "SECRET SANTA" all over green package. *Option: Use computer to print words on green card stock before cutting out package.*

5 Glue mittens near bottom edges of package. Glue package onto Santa.

Finishing Touches

1 Glue pompom to tip of hat.

2 Use toothpick to put glue on back of wiggly eyes. Glue eyes to face.

3 Use gold paint to draw bow and ribbons on package.

Things You'll Need

For each invitation:
- Waterproof tablecloth or plastic trash bags
- 3¼ x 5-inch white invitation card with envelope
- Card stock: red, white, green, pink, blue
- Red-and-white polka-dot paper
- White paper
- 2 (3mm) wiggly eyes
- ¼-inch white pompom
- Paper crimper
- Gold opaque dimensional paint for paper
- Black fine-tip marker or computer with printer
- Craft glue
- Toothpick
- Scissors
- Pencil
- Eraser
- Ruler

Decorations

Santa Snowflakes

Roll the Clay

1 Cover worktable with tablecloth or plastic bags.

2 Squeeze the paper clay with your fingers to make it soft. Pat it into a flat circle.

3 Lay clay circle on wooden board or worktable. Roll it ⅛ inch thick with the rolling pin.

4 Use the cookie cutter to cut an ice-cream cone from clay. Use knife to cut a 1⅝ x ⅝-inch rectangle from clay. Let pieces dry overnight. *Note: Put the rest of the clay in an air-tight container for another project.*

▶ CONTINUED ON PAGE 132

▶CONTINUED FROM PAGE 131

Paint Santa

 Turn clay cone upside down for hat and head.

 For hat, paint 2 inches of pointed end red. Let dry for about 5 minutes.

 Clean brush well with clean water and paper towels. For face, mix a dab of white paint with a dot of pink on a paper plate. Paint round end of cone pink. Let dry.

 Paint the back of the cone in the same way as the front. Let dry.

Put It Together

 For hat brim, glue the clay rectangle over bottom edge of hat. Let dry.

 Brush front of hat and brim with laminating liquid.

 Sprinkle glitter over wet liquid. Let dry. Hold Santa over paper. Tap off extra glitter.

 For mustache, break off the top three "arms" of a 4-inch snowflake. Set two smaller "arms" aside. For beard, glue face over snowflake, covering space that was broken off.

Finishing Touches

 Use toothpick to put a little glue on the back of each eye. Glue eyes to face.

 Glue two small broken pieces of snowflake onto face for mustache. For nose, glue pink pompom between them. Glue ⅜-inch snowflake to tip of hat. Glue star button to hat brim.

Sparkling Snowflakes

 Cover worktable with tablecloth or plastic bags.

 Squeeze the paper clay with your fingers to make it soft. Pat it into a flat circle.

 Lay clay circle on wooden board or worktable. Roll it ⅛ inch thick with the rolling pin.

Things You'll Need

For each Santa:
* ✶ Waterproof tablecloth or plastic trash bags
* ✶ 4-inch glittery plastic snowflake
* ✶ ⅜-inch plastic snowflake
* ✶ White paper clay
* ✶ Small rolling pin or 1-inch wooden dowel
* ✶ Old cutting board (optional)
* ✶ Cookie cutters: 1½-inch rectangle, 3-inch ice-cream cone
* ✶ 2 (7mm) wiggly eyes
* ✶ ⅛-inch pink pompom
* ✶ ½-inch gold star button
* ✶ Fine clear glitter
* ✶ Paper paint: pink, white, red
* ✶ Paintbrush
* ✶ Paper plate
* ✶ Container of water
* ✶ Paper towels
* ✶ Laminating liquid
* ✶ Craft glue
* ✶ Toothpick
* ✶ Ruler

Things You'll Need

* ✶ Waterproof tablecloth or plastic trash bags
* ✶ White paper clay
* ✶ Small rolling pin or 1-inch wooden dowel
* ✶ 2-inch snowflake cookie cutter
* ✶ Fine clear glitter
* ✶ 5mm crystal rhinestones
* ✶ Laminating liquid
* ✶ ½-inch flat brush
* ✶ Toothpick
* ✶ White paper
* ✶ Craft glue
* ✶ Old cutting board (optional)

4 Use the cookie cutter to cut snowflakes from clay. Let snowflakes dry overnight. *Note: Put the rest of the clay in an air-tight container for another project.*

5 Use ½-inch brush to brush front of dry snowflakes with laminating liquid.

6 Sprinkle glitter over wet liquid. Let dry. Hold snowflake over paper. Tap off extra glitter.

7 Use a toothpick to put a drop of craft glue on the back of each rhinestone. Press a rhinestone in the center of each snowflake, at the end of each snowflake arm, and at the bottom of the "V" between each pair of snowflake arms. Let dry.

8 Scatter snowflakes over your party table for extra sparkle. Make them into ornaments by gluing a loop of ⅛-inch ribbon on the back of each one.

Santa Party Cups

Stick Santa to cup using hook-and-loop fastener.

Santa Light Garland

Note: Follow instructions for making Sparkling Snowflakes (page 132), but use a larger 3½-inch snowflake cookie cutter.

1 Glue a clothespin to the back of each Santa Snowflake and Sparkling Snowflake. Make sure openings point to top. Let dry.

2 Clip Santas and snowflakes near lights on cord. Alternate them and space them evenly.

3 Ask an adult to help hang the light string over a doorway or from a mantel.

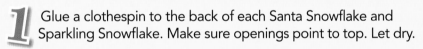

Santa Party Favor Bags

Stick Santa to bag using hook-and-loop fastener. Fill bag with party favors.

Another Idea: Santa Ornaments

Make a Santa ornament by gluing a loop of ⅛-inch ribbon on the back of each Santa Snowflake.

Things You'll Need
For each favor bag:
* Santa Snowflake (see page 131)
* 4½ x 5¾-inch red gift bag with handles
* ½-inch piece adhesive-backed hook-and-loop fastener

Name That Holiday Tune

Have everyone sit in a circle. Ask one person to start the game by humming a Christmas song.

Go around the circle and take turns trying to name the song. If you miss, you are out. The person who names it correctly must hum another song.

Continue taking turns humming and guessing until a song cannot be guessed. The last one humming is the winner.

Blindfolded Art

Give each guest a pencil and piece of plain paper. Have each guest write her name on the back of the paper in tiny letters.

Now turn the paper over. Tie a bandana or scarf over each guest's eyes. While they are blindfolded, have guests draw a picture of Santa.

When the drawings are done, collect the pictures. Then ask your guests to take off the blindfolds.

Without telling who drew each picture, hold up the pictures and have your guests vote on the best. Reveal the winner's name, and give her a small prize.

"'Twas the Night Before Christmas ..."

Have guests sit in a circle. Have them take turns reciting a line from *The Night Before Christmas.* Those who make a mistake are out. The last guest remaining is the winner.

Afterward, read the poem for everyone to enjoy!

Surprise Favors & Prizes

Before your party, wrap several small prizes in plain brown craft paper with red and green string. Place them in a large "Santa sack."

Let each winner choose a prize, but don't open them till all the prizes have been awarded. Then open them together.

If you want, choose a nicer gift to give as a *door prize*. Have each guest write her name on a piece of paper, fold it in quarters, and put it in a bowl. Mix them up, and then have someone pick a name. The winner should open her gift for all to see.

Secret Santa Gift Exchange

On your invitations, ask each guest to bring a wrapped gift. Have them put their name *inside* the package so no one can tell who brought what. Set a price limit — perhaps $5 but no more then $10.

As the guests arrive, write a number on the bottom of each gift with a marker. Write matching numbers on pieces of paper and put them in a bowl.

At the end of the party, have each guest draw a number. Then give them the gift with that number. Before anyone opens her gift, make sure no one has received the present she brought to the party. Have everyone open the exchange gifts together!

Food Fun! Serve a *Santa Face Cake* to your holiday guests. You'll find the recipe and other great food ideas on pages 142–173.

Extra Games & Activities

Add even more fun to your parties by playing some of these extra hilarious and silly games!

Extra Games & Activities

Here's a collection of 12 games sure to add laughs and fun to your party!

Observation Skills

Tell everyone to look around the room while you count to 50 to yourself.

Have everyone leave the room while you make some changes in the room—moving a chair, changing books in the bookcase, changing pictures on the wall, etc.

Then have the guests return. Give them each pencil and paper. Ask them to write down all the changes they see. Whoever notes the most correct changes wins. But wrong answers count against their scores!

Egg Toss

This is a messy outdoor game that can be lots of fun. It is played with raw eggs and teams of two. The object of the game is to see which team can toss an egg the farthest without breaking it.

Start with the first team of two about 5 feet apart. One player tosses the egg to the other, who catches the egg. Then each takes a step backward and tosses the egg again. Each time the egg is tossed and caught successfully, the players take another step back.

When one team breaks its egg, the next team begins. The team that can keep the egg from being broken for the longest distant wins.

Personal History

Give each player a long sheet of paper and a pencil. Have them number from 1 to 16 down the left side.

As you read the list under Column A, have them write answers next to the numbers 1 to 16. Have them write their names at the top of the sheet and exchange papers.

Then, as you read Column B, have each person read the answer to that question on the sheet she is holding. For example, for year of birth, Mary may have written 1860. (That would make her pretty old!)

The answers might make you chuckle!

Column A
1. Any year after 1850
2. Any town
3. Any occupation
4. A sum of money
5. Another sum of money
6. Any bad habit
7. Any good habit
8. Any hobby
9. A number
10. Another number
11. Any color
12. Another color
13. A girl's name
14. A boy's name
15. Some date in the future
16. A number

Column B
1. Year of birth
2. Town where born
3. Occupation
4. Annual income
5. Annual expense
6. Worst fault
7. Best quality
8. Favorite activity
9. Your age
10. Size of shoe
11. Color of eyes
12. Color of hair
13. Your middle name
14. Boyfriend
15. When you will be married
16. Number of kids you will have

The Continuing Story

Give a long sheet of paper and a pencil to one of your guests. Tell her to start a story by writing a sentence. Then fold the paper down so the sentence is covered.

Hand the paper to the next person. Have her write a sentence and fold down the paper.

Continue passing the paper, adding a sentence and folding. When everyone has added a sentence, read the story out loud.

Sir Hinkle Funnyduster

This is a wild and crazy card game. Any number can play, but only one can win.

• The game uses a regular 52-card deck.

• You must be polite and say "Please" and "Thank you."

• The object of the game is to end up with all the cards.

Deal out all the cards.

The person to the left of the dealer starts by asking any player for a kind of card—but the person must say "Please" before asking for the card. For example: "Dawn, please give me all your 3's."

A player must say "Thank you" before touching the cards being received.

If anyone forgets to say "Please" or "Thank you," *any* player may say, "Sir Hinkle Funnyduster!" The first person to say "Sir Hinkle Funnyduster" gets *all* the cards from the person who forgot to say "Please" or "Thank you."

Here is an example of how the game might go. Suppose Mary is first. She might say, "Chris, please give me all of your kings." Chris has two kings, so she gives them to Mary. Mary must say "Thank you" before touching the cards. Mary continues to ask for other cards from anyone.

Mary's turn is over when a player does not have a card she asks for. The person to Mary's left goes next.

Players who lose their cards may talk to anyone; but *a person with cards* may not talk to *a person without cards*. If a player with cards talks to someone without cards, anyone may say "Sir Hinkle Funnyduster" and get that person's cards.

Again, the person receiving the cards must say "Thank you" before touching the cards.

The player with all the cards at the end wins!

Variety Toss

Nail several different tin cans from biggest to littlest to a length of board. Assign numbers to the cans.

Prop the board at an angle with the smallest can farthest from the players.

From a set distance, players take turns tossing pennies or washers into the cans. Whoever gets the most points wins.

Seven Sticks

• Each side begins with Seven sticks about a foot long.

• Choose an area outdoors about 20 x 40 feet. Place a marker in each corner, then place a string across to divide the area in half. Each side of the marked area belongs to a team. Set up jails about 6 feet square in opposite back corners. Lay sticks or other objects to mark the borders of the jails.

• The object of the game is to end up with all 14 sticks.

Choose up sides with equal numbers on both sides. The opposing players try to "steal" sticks from the opposite side without being touched. Once a player touches a stick, she takes the stick back to her team's pile.

If an opposing player touches someone in their territory before that player touches a stick, the player caught goes to jail. The only way a captured player can get out of jail is for a teammate to come into enemy territory and touch her hand before being touched by the enemy. If a player is touched before touching a teammate in jail, she also goes to jail.

A team wins when it has all 14 sticks.

Ring Toss

Ask an adult to cut five 17-inch pieces of stiff rope. Tape the ends together to make rings.

Stick a stake or dowel into the ground.

Mark a line for tossing the rings. The player tossing the most rings over the pin wins.

Clown Toss

Ask an adult to saw a hole in the center of a half-sheet of plywood. Draw or paint a clown face so that the hole is the clown's mouth.

Prop up the clown and toss beanbags or tennis balls through the clown's mouth.

Funniest Sentence

Give guests paper and pencil. Have them write the funniest sentence they can using these six words: *nose, tree, mouse, door, close, purple.*

The sentence can be long or short, but it must use all six words. When everyone is finished, collect papers and read sentences out loud.

"El" Quiz

Give your guests paper and pencil. Have them number the paper from 1 to 12. Explain that each of the answers is a word that begins with "el."

1. What "el" takes you up and brings you down?
2. What "el" names the president?
3. What "el" is a joint?
4. What "el" is an odd number?
5. What "el" is older?
6. What "el" is romantic?
7. What "el" is at the circus?
8. What "el" is a kind of deer and also a club?
9. What "el" gets rid of most things?
10. What "el" gives you the most light?
11. What "el" lives in the woods?
12. What "el" is the grandest?

Answers:

1. elevator
2. election
3. elbow
4. eleven
5. elder
6. elopement
7. elephant
8. elk
9. eliminate
10. electricity
11. elm
12. elegant

Guess the State Abbreviation

1. The most religious state?
2. The most egotistical?
3. Not a state for the untidy.
4. The father of states?
5. The most maidenlike?
6. The most useful for cutting grass?
7. Best in time of flood?
8. The number state?
9. State of exclamation?
10. The doctor's state?
11. No such word as fail?
12. Most unhealthy state?
13. The mining state?
14. The tricky state?

(Mass.)
(Me.)
(Wash.)
(Pa.)
(Miss.)
(Mo.)
(Ark.)
(Tenn.)
(Oh.)
(Md.)
(Kan.)
(Ill.)
(Ore.)
(Conn.)

Food Fun

Kids will have a blast in the kitchen with these easy recipes! This food is as fun to make as it is to eat!

Food Fun—Meals

Treat your party guests to delicious and filling food that you've made yourself!

Cookie Cutter Sandwiches

Things You'll Need
* 4 slices lunch meat such as ham, bologna or turkey
* 4 slices American cheese
* 4 pieces bread
* Pickles for garnish
* Cookie cutters
* Cutting board
* Plate

1 Put a slice of meat and a slice of cheese on the cutting board.

2 Use a cookie cutter to cut a shape—a heart, a star, etc.— from the center of each slice. Save the outsides of the shapes.

3 Put slices of bread on plate. Lay meat and cheese slices on bread in a pretty arrangement. Add pickles to decorate the plate.

Ham Roll-Ups

1 Trim the ends from the green onions.

2 Lay ham slices on a cutting board. Spread ham with cream cheese. Lay a green onion on the cream cheese on each slice.

3 Roll up the ham slices. Chill in the refrigerator until the cream cheese is firm.

4 Cut rolls into slices before serving.

Things You'll Need
* 1 package sliced ham
* 1 package softened cream cheese
* Green onions, washed and cleaned
* Cutting board
* Knife

Sandwich Faces

Use your imagination and make up faces ahead of time. Or let your party guests make their own faces during your party. Try these ideas, or come up with your own.

Lay a cooked hamburger patty on slice of bread or half a bun. Cut a face from cheese. Make pickle ears, catsup nose and mouth, green pepper eyebrows, and olive eyes.

Decorate sloppy joes with grated cheese hair, olive eyes, green pepper mouth and eyebrows, and mushroom nose and ears.

Canoe Sandwich

1 Pull the soft bread out of the center of the roll with your fingers.

Things You'll Need
* French roll or hoagie bun
* Softened butter or margarine
* Your favorite sandwich filling: peanut butter, chicken salad, sliced meat or cheese, etc.
* Knife

2 Butter the insides of the roll.

3 Fill with your choice of sandwich filling.

Pumpkin Pizzas

1 Split the English muffin in half. Toast both pieces lightly in the toaster.

2 Spread a generous tablespoon of crushed tomatoes on top of each toasted muffin half. Sprinkle it with salt, pepper, dried oregano and granulated garlic.

3 Put three slices of pepperoni on top. Cover them with a slice of American cheese. Add slices of black olive for the eyes and nose. Use a piece cut from a slice of green pepper for the stem. Use a slice of red pepper for the mouth.

4 Ask an adult to preheat the oven to 375 degrees. Cover the baking sheet with heavy-duty aluminum foil. Place pumpkin pizzas on the foil.

5 Using pot holders, carefully put the pan in the hot oven. Let bake for 8–10 minutes, or until the cheese is melted.

6 Ask an adult to carefully remove the hot pan from the oven. Use a spatula to move the hot pizzas from the cookie sheet to a serving tray.

Things You'll Need
* English muffins
* Crushed tomatoes
* Salt
* Pepper
* Granulated garlic
* Dried oregano
* Individual slices of American cheese
* Sliced pepperoni
* Sliced black olives
* Sliced green and red bell pepper
* Spatula
* Spoon
* Heavy-duty aluminum foil
* Baking sheet
* Pot holder
* Knife
* Cutting board
* Toaster
* Oven
* Serving tray

Tortilla Pinwheels

1 Spread a thin layer of cream cheese all over one side of tortilla.

2 Cover cream cheese with thin layer of meat slices.

3 Roll up tortilla. Cut roll into 1-inch slices. Stick a toothpick through each slice to hold it together.

Things You'll Need
* Flour tortillas
* Thin slices of ham, turkey or lunch meat
* Spreadable cream cheese— plain or chive-and-onion
* Toothpicks or party picks

Other Ideas

Add washed, dried spinach leaves to your roll-ups for extra color.

Serve sparkling apple cider or fruit juice in plastic champagne glasses. Float a washed fresh strawberry in each glass.

Cottage Cheese & Salsa Omelet

Note: Always ask an adult to help you when using the stove.

1 Heat skillet on the stovetop at medium heat.

2 Mix eggs, milk and salt in bowl with fork. Blend until frothy.

3 Pour eggs into heated skillet. Watch closely, and adjust heat if needed. When omelet is brown and firm on the bottom, sprinkle cheeses over half the omelet. Cover with lid until cheese begins to melt.

4 Remove lid. Drizzle 1 Tablespoon of salsa over melted cheese. Fold omelet in half with spatula.

5 Use spatula to place omelet on plate. Top with remaining 1 Tablespoon of salsa. Season with pepper.

Things You'll Need
For each omelet:
* Plastic wrap
* 2 eggs
* 3 Tablespoons milk
* ¼ cup 2% cottage cheese
* 2 Tablespoons grated cheddar cheese
* 2 Tablespoons mild or medium salsa
* ¼ teaspoon salt
* Pepper to taste
* Mixing bowl *and* fork
* Small nonstick skillet with lid
* Spatula
* Plate

Penguin Tuna Sandwiches

Things You'll Need
* Sliced bread
* Softened butter
* Tuna fish
* Mayonnaise
* Olives stuffed with pimiento
* Large fish cookie cutter
* Knife
* Cutting board

1 Cut fish from bread slices with cookie cutter.

2 Spread one side of each slice with softened butter.

3 Mix tuna fish and mayonnaise together. Spread tuna fish on buttered side of one fish. Place another fish on top, having butter on inside.

4 For eyes, cut olives into thin slices. Place a slice on each fish sandwich.

Mini PB & Honey Sandwiches

Trim the crusts from peanut butter and honey sandwiches and cut them into small squares.

Diva Dogs & Dips

Note: *Always ask an adult to help you when using the oven.*

1 Preheat oven to 350 degrees. Cut hot dogs lengthwise into four equal pieces.

2 Unroll refrigerated crescent rolls. Do not pull apart into triangles. Pat the rolls together along lines.

3 Cut roll dough into 1-inch strips. Wrap a strip around each piece of hot dog.

4 Place on ungreased cookie sheet. Spray tops with non-stick cooking spray.

5 Bake in oven according to directions on crescent roll package.

6 Serve sauces and dips in cupcake liners.

Things You'll Need
* Refrigerated crescent rolls
* Hot dogs
* Your favorite sauces, dips and dressings (barbecue sauce, catsup, mustard, ranch dressing, etc.)
* Cupcake liners
* Knife
* Cookie sheet
* Oven
* Non-stick cooking spray
* Pot holders

Dogs in Blankets

Note: *Always ask an adult to help you when using the oven.*

1 Preheat the oven to 375 degrees. While it is heating, cut crusts off bread. Roll bread flat with rolling pin. Set aside.

2 Boil hot dogs until plump. Drain off water.

3 Place a flattened bread slice on cutting board. Place cheese on top of bread. Lay cooked hot dog along one edge and roll up tightly in bread.

4 Hold bread in place with toothpicks. Place on foil-lined baking sheet.

5 Repeat with other hot dogs.

6 Bake for 10–15 minutes. Cheese should be bubbly and bread should be browned.

7 Ask an adult to remove the hot pan from oven using pot holders. Let cool slightly before serving.

Things You'll Need
* Hot dogs
* Whole wheat bread
* Cheese slices
* Long toothpicks
* Baking sheet lined with foil
* Cutting board and knife
* Rolling pin
* Oven
* Pot holders

Mini Pizza Bites

Note: *Always ask an adult to help you when using the oven.*

Things You'll Need

★ Mini pita pockets *or* English muffins, cut in half
★ Pizza sauce
★ Sliced pepperoni
★ Grated mozzarella and cheddar cheese
★ Thinly sliced veggies (optional)
★ Pizza pan or foil-lined baking sheet
★ Spoon
★ Pizza cutter
★ Oven
★ Pot holder

1 Preheat the oven to 400 degrees. While it is heating, place pita pockets or muffin halves on pan or baking sheet.

2 Place a spoonful of sauce on each pita or muffin half. Spread it around.

3 Add slices of pepperoni and veggies.

4 Sprinkle each pizza with cheese.

5 Place in oven and bake about 8 minutes. Cheese should be bubbling.

6 Ask an adult to remove the hot pan from oven using pot holders. Cut pizzas into small wedges.

Mini Pizza Pies

Note: *Always ask an adult to help you when using the oven.*

1 Preheat oven to 375 degrees.

2 Separate dough into individual biscuits. Pinch dough between fingers and thumbs to form a larger circle with edges slightly higher, like a pizza. Place dough on cookie sheet.

3 Pour one large spoonful of sauce on dough. Spread around with spoon. Place toppings on dough in this order: meat, veggies, fruit and cheese.

4 Have an adult help you bake pizzas in oven for 15 minutes or until crust is lightly browned.

5 Remove from oven and serve while hot.

Things You'll Need

★ 2 large cookie sheets
★ Prepared biscuit dough*
★ Pizza tomato sauce
★ Shredded cheese: cheddar, mozzarella
★ Meat: pepperoni, cooked hamburger or sausage, ham, shrimp
★ Toppings: onions, mushrooms, olives, peppers, pineapple
★ Large tablespoon
★ Pizza cutter

*Pillsbury Buttermilk Biscuits were used in this project.

LET'S HAVE A PARTY! ● Food Fun

Flower Sandwiches

For each sandwich, cut two flowers from bread with cookie cutters. Use small round cookie cutter to cut center from one flower. Set aside.

Egg Salad Sandwiches

 Slice cooked eggs. Put them in a bowl and mash with a fork.

 Add desired amount of sandwich dressing. Season with salt, pepper and green onion.

 Spread a heaping tablespoon of egg salad on one bread flower. Top with another bread flower with hole cut out.

Cheese Sandwiches

 Lightly butter one side of each bread flower.

 Spread cheese over butter on bottom flower shape, keeping it inside the flower. Top with bread flower with hole cut out, butter side down.

Nut Butter and Jelly Sandwiches

 Spread nut butter on bread flower.

Spread jelly over nut butter. Top with bread flower with hole cut out.

Serve With a Smile!

Arrange flower sandwiches in pretty rows on a serving tray.

Experiment with making other kinds of sandwiches. The filling will show through the center of the flower.

Things You'll Need

* Flower-shaped cookie cutter
* Small round cookie cutter
* Bread slices with crusts trimmed off
* Nut butters: almond, peanut, cashew
* Jams or jellies
* Margarine or butter
* Thinly sliced or grated cheddar cheese
* Cream cheese
* Hard-cooked eggs
* Sandwich dressing
* Green onion, finely chopped
* Salt and pepper
* Mixing bowl
* Forks, knives and spoons
* Cutting board
* Serving tray

Food Fun—Snacks

You and your friends won't know which is more fun—making these snacks or eating them!

Fruit Kabobs

1 Cut smaller fruits in half. Slice larger fruit.

2 Thread pieces of fruit on skewers and arrange them on a plate.

Things You'll Need
* Colorful fruit such as seedless grapes, strawberries, cantaloupe, peaches, pineapples or oranges
* Short wooden skewers (Don't use ones with sharp points)

Things You'll Need
* 1 bunch of celery
* Smooth or chunky peanut butter
* Cream cheese
* Raisins or dried cranberries
* Sharp knife
* Table knife

Ant Logs

  Cut ends off celery. Wash celery under running cold water.

  Put celery on plate. Fill grooves in celery with peanut butter or cream cheese.

  Stick raisins in the filling for black ants or dried cranberries for red ants.

Painted Toast

  Place a few drops of each food coloring into separate cups. Add ¼ cup of milk to each cup and stir.

  Use paintbrushes to decorate bread with designs, faces, or pictures.

  Toast bread and serve or make part of a sandwich.

Things You'll Need
* Bread
* Food coloring
* Milk
* Toaster
* Clean, unused paintbrushes
* Cups
* Measuring cups

Sports-Fan Snack

1 Pour popcorn in large bowl. Melt butter or margarine in saucepan. Stir in honey, lemon peel and cinnamon. Sprinkle mixture over popcorn.

2 Add raisins, apricots, and peanuts. Mix well.

3 Serve immediately or store in plastic bags. Makes about 2½ quarts.

Things You'll Need
* 2 quarts popped popcorn
* 1½ cups golden raisins
* 1½ cups dry-roasted peanuts
* 2 Tablespoons butter or margarine
* 1 Tablespoon grated lemon peel
* ¼ cup honey
* 1½ cups diced dried apricots
* ¼ teaspoon cinnamon
* Large bowl
* Spoon
* Small saucepan
* Self-sealing plastic bags
* Stove

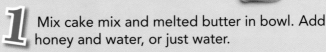

Things You'll Need
* 1 box white cake mix
* 1 stick (½ cup) melted butter or margarine
* 1 Tablespoon honey (optional)
* 2 Tablespoons water
* Bright crunchy snacks such as Fruity Pebbles, Fruit Loops, Trix, M&M's
* Raisins, peanuts, candy bits
* Coconut
* Food coloring
* Mixing bowl
* Rubber scraper

Edible Clay

1 Mix cake mix and melted butter in bowl. Add honey and water, or just water.

2 Use your hands to mix and knead dough until it's smooth and sticky.

3 Add food coloring to make different colors. Mix coloring with small amounts of dough.

4 Form creatures and objects by making balls, snakes or flat shapes. Add eyes and other decorations using some of the crunchy treats.

Edible Putty

Wash hands. Mix ingredients together. Divide into portions for guests to make animals, creatures or other objects.

Things You'll Need
* 4 cups dried milk powder
* 3½ cups honey
* 4 cups powdered sugar
* 3½ cups peanut butter

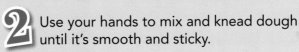

Banana Dog

Things You'll Need
* Hot dog bun
* Peanut butter
* Jelly
* Banana

1 Open hot dog bun. Spread one side with peanut butter and the other side with jelly.

2 Peel banana and put it in bun. Eat like hot dog.

Wormy Apples

Note: Always ask an adult to help you when using the oven.

1 Cut out center of apples. Place on cookie sheet and fill with Red Hots.

2 Bake for 35–40 minutes at 350 degrees. Remove from oven and top with gummy worms.

Things You'll Need
* Apples
* Red Hots candies
* Gummy worms
* Knife
* Cookie sheet

Veggie Platter with Lemon Dill Dip

Things You'll Need
* Assorted peeled, cleaned fresh vegetables: carrots, cucumbers, celery, cherry tomatoes, pepper slices, etc.
* ½ cup low-fat plain yogurt
* ½ cup low-fat sour cream
* 1½ teaspoons dried dill
* Grated rind of 1 small lemon
* 1 Tablespoon freshly squeezed lemon juice
* ½ teaspoon salt
* Mixing bowl and spoon
* Knife or serrated cutters
* Cutting board
* Serving tray
* Bowl for dip
* Plastic wrap

1 The day before your party:
Make dip by mixing yogurt, sour cream, dill, lemon rind, juice and salt together.

2 Pour dip into serving bowl. Cover bowl with plastic wrap. Store in refrigerator.

3 Cut vegetables into finger-sized servings. Try cutting carrots and cucumbers on an angle with a serrated cutter.

Just before your party:
Place dip bowl in center of tray. Arrange vegetables around it in colorful rows.

Crisp, Cold Veggie Tray

Arrange rows of veggies in a large flower shape.

Fresh Fruit with Yogurt Cream

1 Mix yogurt, pudding and whipped cream in mixing bowl. Pour into smaller bowl. Set it in center of tray, or off to one side.

2 Arrange fruit on tray around bowl of dip.

3 For decoration, add lime slices around tray.

Things You'll Need
* Fresh fruit, cleaned and cut into bite-size pieces: apple, strawberries, raspberries, pineapple, mango, papaya, banana
* Lime slices for garnish
* 1 cup low-fat French vanilla yogurt
* ½ cup low-fat vanilla pudding
* ½ cup real whipped cream
* Grated coconut (optional)
* Mixing bowl and spoon
* Serving tray
* Small bowl

Things You'll Need
* Chocolates covered with white dots
* Chocolate kisses in silver wrap
* Fish-shaped crackers and pretzels
* Gummy fish

South Pole Snacks

Set out bowls of candies and snacks that remind you of ice, snow or the ocean.

S'mores

Place a regular marshmallow on top of a graham cracker. Top with four or five chocolate chips or a small square of a chocolate bar. Place another graham cracker on top and set on a microwave-safe plate.

Microwave each s'more for about 7 seconds, until marshmallow puffs up and chocolate melts. Or, place s'mores on a foil-lined baking sheet. Bake at 350 degrees until marshmallows have softened and chocolate melts—about 15 minutes.

Be careful. They are hot!

Mini Fruit & Dip

Cut fruit into small squares or use scoop to make small balls. Insert a party toothpick in each piece of fruit.

For dip, mix one jar of marshmallow cream with one 8-ounce package of softened cream cheese. Cut up cherries into small bits and mix into dip. Add a small amount of cherry juice for color and flavor.

Music Munching Mix

Let's Begin
Mix all ingredients in a bowl.

Another Idea
Fill plastic sandwich bags with Music Munching Mix for your guests to take home.

Things You'll Need
* Cheddar-flavored popped corn
* Raisins
* Golden raisins
* Cashews
* Honey-nut O-shaped oat cereal
* Candy-coated peanut butter candies
* Banana chips
* Miniature pretzel twists

Cheese & Fruit Tray

Use a small flower cookie cutter to cut flower shapes from thin slices of cheese. Try different kinds of cheese to get different colors and textures. If the cheese sticks, dip the cutter in hot water and quickly dry it before cutting.

Arrange cheese flowers on tray with fruit. Try grapes, melon slices, strawberries and fresh blueberries.

Floral Crudités & Dip

Check your library or cookbooks for directions on cutting vegetables into fancy shapes. Or, cut fresh, washed vegetables into slices or chunks. Try carrots, celery, mushrooms, tomatoes, radishes, broccoli, cauliflower and peppers.

Arrange vegetables in pretty rows on a serving tray. Add a cup of dip. (Buy it, or make your favorite recipe.)

Several hours before serving, clean and trim a few green onions. Cut fringes in the green end. Put them in a bowl of ice water. The green fringes will curl up. Add these to your tray for a pretty garnish.

Chocolate-Dipped Strawberries

1 Wash strawberries and let dry

2 Melt chocolate chips in microwave following manufacturer's directions

3 Dip strawberries in chocolate and set on wax paper. Sprinkle with sugar crystals.

4 Refrigerate until chocolate is set.

Things You'll Need
* White chocolate chips
* Whole strawberries
* Pink sugar crystals
* Waxed paper

Food Fun—Desserts

No party is complete without dessert! Here are lots of great recipes to satisfy your sweet tooth!

Cupcake Cones

1 Cut bottoms from egg carton. Turn upside-down. Set cones upright in it while you fill them with the batter.

2 Mix cake mix, eggs and pie filling in a bowl using a mixer or spoon.

3 Spoon the batter into the cones, filling them ⅔ full.

4 Remove one cone from egg carton and set it in the microwave. Microwave for 30–40 seconds. Let cone stand for 2–3 minutes in the microwave.

5 Use a pot holder to carefully take the cone out of the microwave. Repeat with the other cones.

Things You'll Need

* 1 egg carton
* Flat-bottom ice-cream cones
* 18-ounce package cake mix
* 2 eggs
* 21-ounce can pie filling
* Mixing bowl
* Mixer or spoon
* Rubber scraper
* Microwave

Girlfriend Cupcakes

Let's Begin!

Decorate frosted cupcakes with "girlfriend chatter" using the gel or frosting—"Sweet," "Cute," "Funny," "Silly," "Chatty," "Giving," "Artsy," "Dancer," "Diva," "Girly Girl," "Groovy," "Chic," "Sporty," etc.

Things You'll Need

* Baked cupcakes frosted with white frosting
* Tubes of cake-decorating gel or canned frosting with decorator tips

Heart Cake

Things You'll Need
* ✶ White cake mix plus ingredients to make it
* ✶ Frosting and decorations
* ✶ 9-inch round cake pan
* ✶ 9-inch square cake pan
* ✶ Pot holders
* ✶ Mixer
* ✶ Mixing bowl
* ✶ Spoon
* ✶ Rubber scraper
* ✶ Cooling rack

1 Ask an adult to preheat the oven to the temperature listed for your pan size on the box of cake mix.

2 Mix the cake batter following the instructions on the box of cake mix.

3 Grease and flour the cake pan. Pour half the batter in each pan. Bake following the instructions on the box.

4 Ask an adult to take the hot cakes out of the oven and tip them out of the pans, onto a cooling rack. Let cakes cool completely.

5 Cut the round cake in half. Place the cut sides against two sides of the square cake to form a heart.

6 Frost and decorate the cake as you choose.

Giant Kiss

Things You'll Need
* ✶ 9-inch round cake pan
* ✶ 5 cups crisp rice cereal
* ✶ ¼ cup margarine or butter
* ✶ 10-ounce package marshmallows or 4 cups miniature marshmallows
* ✶ Large bowl
* ✶ Spoon
* ✶ Kitchen funnel
* ✶ Measuring cup
* ✶ Plastic wrap
* ✶ Saucepan
* ✶ Stove

1 Melt the margarine in the saucepan over low heat. *Note: Always have an adult close by when using the stove.* Add marshmallows and stir until they are completely melted. Cook for 3 more minutes, stirring constantly.

2 Remove the pan from the heat. Add the cereal and stir until it is coated with the mixture. Let the mixture cool slightly.

3 Coat the funnel and your fingers with margarine. Press the cereal mixture into the funnel, then pop out to cool.

4 Wrap cooled kiss in plastic wrap. Makes 2–4 kisses.

Star & Moon Cookies

1 Roll out cookie dough ¼–⅓ inch thick. Cut with cookie cutters. Move cookies to cookie sheet with spatula.

2 Stick end lollipop sticks into some cookies to use on centerpiece or to serve as cookie pops. Leave some cookies without sticks.

3 Ask an adult to preheat oven to correct temperature. Bake cookies as directed. Ask an adult to remove pan from oven using pot holders. Let cool.

4 Frost moon cookies with yellow. Frost star cookies with blue. Sprinkle cookies with sugars or sprinkles.

Moon & Stars Cake

Press cooled, iced moon and star cookies into icing on top and sides of your favorite layer cake.

Other Ideas

Serve your cookies and cake with milk or hot chocolate with marshmallows. Pretzels and cut-up vegetables with French onion dip make great slumber party snacks, too!

Things You'll Need
* Sugar cookie dough
* Lollipop sticks
* Frosting: blue, yellow
* Colored sugars or sprinkles
* Rolling pin
* Spatula
* Cookie cutters: star, moon
* Cookie sheet lined with baking parchment
* Oven
* Pot holders
* Cooling rack

Deep Sea Gelatin

1 Ask an adult to help you make the gelatin, following the instructions on the package.

2 Chill gelatin in refrigerator until it begins to thicken. Pour into clear glass bowl.

3 Push fish candies down into gelatin using toothpick or kabob stick. The fish should look like they are swimming in the gelatin.

Things You'll Need
* Large box blue gelatin
* Fish-shaped "gummy" candies
* Glass measuring cup
* Saucepan
* Mixing bowl
* Timer
* Spoon or wire whisk
* Clear glass bowl
* Toothpick or kabob stick

Graham Cracker Bars

1 Ask an adult to preheat the oven to 350 degrees.

2 Unwrap the stick of butter and put it in the pan. Stick it in the oven while it is heating up. Leave it in just long enough for the butter to melt.

3 Tilt the pan to cover the bottom with a layer of melted butter. Sprinkle the graham cracker crumbs evenly over the melted butter. Pour the sweetened condensed milk right from the can, all over the crumbs.

4 Sprinkle the chocolate chips, coconut and nuts evenly over the sweetened condensed milk. Press it down lightly with the palm of your hand.

5 Using pot holders, carefully put the pan on the middle rack of the hot oven. Bake for 25 minutes, or until light brown.

6 Ask an adult to remove the hot pan from the oven. Let it cool completely. Cut the cookies into bars.

Things You'll Need
* 1 bunch of celery
* 1½ cups graham cracker crumbs
* 14-ounce can sweetened condensed milk
* 1 stick (½ cup) butter or margarine
* 1 cup chocolate chips
* 1 cup chopped nuts
* 1⅓ cups flaked coconut
* 13 x 9-inch baking pan
* Pot holders
* Mixing bowl
* Spoon
* Rubber scraper
* Knife

Things You'll Need
* Baked cupcakes
* White frosting
* Chocolate frosting
* Chocolate chips
* Orange fruit roll-up
* Small knife or spatula
* Toothpick
* Cutting board

Penguin Cupcakes

1 For penguin face, use toothpick to draw a heart in center of cupcake. Use spatula to spread white frosting in heart shape

2 Spread rest of cupcake with chocolate frosting.

3 For beak, unroll fruit roll-up on cutting board. Cut a small triangle. Press beak onto face (see photo).

4 For eyes, press two chocolate chips onto face.

Tiny Cupcakes

Prepare cake mix of any flavor. Pour batter into small candy cup papers. Bake for less time than required for regular-size cupcakes.

Sugared Ballet Slipper Cookies

Note: *Instead of shoes, cut the cookie dough into star shapes and serve to your "guest stars"!*

 1 Using pattern on page 178, cut an oval from cardboard. Using cardboard pattern, cut ovals from rolled-out cookie dough. Bake according to recipe or package instructions. Let cool.

2 Frost cookies to look like ballet shoes.

3 Decorate frosted cookies with your choice of sprinkles, colored sugar or other edible decorations.

Things You'll Need
* Dough for your favorite homemade sugar cookies or tube of refrigerated sugar cookie dough, rolled about ¼ inch thick
* Homemade pink icing or ready-made pink icing in a tub or can
* Assorted sprinkles, pink sugar, edible glitter, etc.
* Cardboard
* Small sharp knife

Rainbow Gelatin Cubes

Using a pastry brush, lightly oil a square glass or metal pan.

Follow instructions on box to make gelatin. Pour it into the pan and set it in the refrigerator until firm.

Repeat to make different flavors.

Cut gelatin into cubes. Dip bottom of pan into warm water and tip cubes out into a bowl.

Dainty Sugar Cookies

Prepare sugar cookie dough or purchase prepared dough. Roll out dough and cut shapes with small star, moon, flower or heart cookie cutters. Sprinkle with "fairy dust" sugar sprinkles.

Glamour Cookies

Things You'll Need

★ 1 recipe Sugar Cookies (recipe follows)
★ Cookie cutters
★ 1 recipe Icing (see page 161)
★ Food coloring
★ Decorator icing bags with No. 2 tip

Sugar Cookies

★ 2 sticks butter
★ 1 cup sugar
★ 1 egg
★ 1 teaspoon vanilla
★ 2 teaspoons baking powder
★ 3 cups flour
★ Mixer with large bowl
★ Another medium bowl
★ Rubber scraper
★ Rolling sheet or cutting board
★ Rolling pin
★ Cookie sheet
★ Cookie cutters
★ Cooling rack

1 Ask an adult to preheat the oven to 400 degrees.

2 In the mixer bowl, blend the butter and sugar at medium speed until it's smooth, creamy and lighter in color.

3 Beat in the egg and vanilla.

4 In the medium bowl, mix the baking powder and flour. Add it to the creamed mixture in the mixer bowl 1 cup at a time. Mix it well before adding the next cup. Stop the mixer once in a while and scrape down the sides of the bowl with a scraper.

5 When all the flour and baking powder has been added and mixed in, spoon the dough onto a rolling sheet or board that has been sprinkled lightly with flour. Form the dough into a big ball with your hands. Then pat it to flatten it slightly. If the dough seems too soft or sticky, put it back in the bowl. Cover it with plastic wrap and let it sit in the refrigerator for 30 minutes or so.

6 Use the roller to roll the dough about ¼–½ inch thick.

7 Cut dough with cookie cutters that have been dipped in flour. Use a spatula to carefully move the cookies to an ungreased cookie sheet.

8 Using pot holders, carefully put the sheet on the center rack of the oven. Bake for 5–6 minutes, or until the edges just get golden brown.

9 Ask an adult to take the hot cookie sheet out of the oven. Set it on a cooling rack.

10 Let the cookies cool on the pan for a minute. Then use a spatula to carefully move them to a cooling rack. Let cookies cool completely before icing them.

Edible Flower Cupcakes

Make or buy your favorite cupcakes.

Decorate cupcakes with clean, dry edible flowers from the grocery store's produce department. You can use lavender, violets, pansies or carnations.

Check your local library or the Internet for more information about edible flowers. Have an adult help you. *Not all flowers are edible. Some flowers are toxic.*

It is safest to use flowers from the produce department. Even some "edible" flowers can make you sick if they have been sprayed with fertilizer or insecticide.

To sugar the flowers before you put them on the cupcakes: Use a paintbrush to brush the edges of the petals with egg white. Sprinkle with extra-fine granulated sugar (or berry sugar). Let dry for a short while.

Store decorated cupcakes in the refrigerator until serving.

Another Idea: Decorate with Candy

Decorate cupcakes with candy or gummy flowers and butterflies.

Frosted Butterfly Sugar Cookies

Make or purchase your favorite sugar cookie dough. Roll out dough and cut with butterfly or flower cookie cutters.

Before baking, sprinkle the cookies with granulated or colored sugar.

Or, after cookies are baked and cooled, decorate them with brightly colored icings.

Icing

1 Mix all the ingredients in a mixer bowl. Beat at low speed for 7–10 minutes, until the icing forms peaks when you dip a spoon into it and pull it back out. Add food coloring, if you want.

2 Using the No. 2 top, pipe icing around the edges of the cookies. **Note:** *Ask an adult to help with this step.*

3 Thin the remaining icing with a little water, adding it a tablespoon at a time. Fill in top of cookie, letting icing flow to edges.

Things You'll Need
* 2 sticks butter
* 3 Tablespoons meringue powder
* 4 cups icing sugar
* 1 cup solid vegetable shortening
* 6 Tablespoons water
* Mixer with large bowl
* Icing bag with a No. 2 tip

Kitty Cupcakes

Things You'll Need
* Baked cupcakes in yellow and blue paper cupcake holders
* Tub of pink frosting
* Tubes of icing: white, pink
* Pink craft foam
* Craft glue
* Blue M&M's
* Pull-apart red licorice strips
* Orange jelly beans
* Small clean scissors
* Toothpicks

1 Frost cupcake with pink frosting.

2 Press jelly bean in center of cupcake for nose. Cut six short strips of red licorice for whiskers. Press three to face on each side of nose. Press M&M's onto cupcake for eyes.

3 Cut two small triangles from pink craft foam for ears. Break toothpick in half; glue broken end to back of each ear. Let glue dry.

4 Squeeze pink icing onto craft foam to make insides of ears. Stick ears into cupcake.

5 Squeeze dots of white icing onto blue eyes for highlights.

Gelatin Cups

Note: *Ask for an adult's help in using the stove.*

Things You'll Need
* Large box gelatin
* 2 cups water
* 2 cups clear apple juice
* Saucepan
* Stove
* Spoon
* 4- to 8-ounce clear plastic cups
* Soccer spoons
* Whipped topping in a can

1 Pour water in saucepan. Bring to a boil. Pour gelatin powder into a bowl.

2 Pour hot water into powder. Stir for at least 2 minutes.

3 Pour apple juice into gelatin. Stir to mix.

4 Set plastic cups on tray. Pour gelatin into cups. Refrigerate until thick enough to hold up a plastic spoon.

5 Stand a decorated soccer spoon (page 73) in the middle of each cup. Top with whipped topping. Refrigerate until ready to serve.

Flip-Flop Crispy Cakes

1 Lay flip-flop pattern (page 181) on top of fruit roll-up. Cut out using a sharp knife.

2 Press fruit shape onto Crispy Cake. Use a knife to cut around the edge. Carefully lift off pan onto plate. Press to reshape cake into the shape of a flip-flop.

3 Use the point of the knife to make holes through the fruit roll-up and crispy cake where shown by the dot and the x's on the pattern.

4 Cut licorice in half. Stick the ends into the holes in the crispy cake to look like straps. Press cake tightly around licorice to hold it.

Things You'll Need
* One recipe of Crispy Cake (recipe follows)
* Fruit roll-ups
* Black licorice
* Knife

Crispy Cake

Things You'll Need
* 1 package marshmallows
* 3 Tablespoons butter or margarine
* 6 cups crisp rice cereal
* Cooking spray
* Heat-proof spoon
* Scraper
* Pot holders

1 Put the marshmallows and margarine in a microwave bowl. Heat on HIGH power for 2 minutes.

2 Using pot holders, carefully remove the bowl from the microwave. Stir the margarine and marshmallow.

3 Put the bowl back in the microwave. Microwave on HIGH for 1 minute longer.

4 Using pot holders, carefully remove the bowl from the microwave. Stir until smooth.

5 Stir cereal into bowl. Stir until well coated.

6 Spray a 13 x 9-inch pan with cooking spray. Press warm mixture into pan. Let set until firm.

Monkey Cupcakes

Painting

1 Cover worktable with tablecloth or plastic bags.

2 Paint ¾-inch circles (ears) and 1¼-inch circle (face) pink. Paint 2-inch circle (head) red. Let dry.

Face & Details

1 Use a pencil to trace the pattern for monkey's face (below) onto white paper.

2 Turn paper over. Trace over the lines you traced in step 1.

3 Turn the pattern right side up again. Lay it on the pink face. Trace over the pattern lines again with a pencil. The lines will now be on the pink circle.

4 Dip a dry paintbrush in red paint. Wipe the paint off on a paper towel until almost no more color comes off the brush. Now wipe the brush in a circle on monkey's cheeks.

5 To paint the cheek dots, dip the tip of your paintbrush handle into white paint. Touch it to the face. Let dry.

6 Using the fine tip of the black marker, draw details on monkey's face. Use the bullet tip of the black marker to draw eyes.

7 Use the fine tip of the black marker to draw details on ears. Draw outline around red circle, close to edge.

Put It Together

1 Glue the face to the head. Glue the ears to the back side of the head. Glue the head to the wide end of the craft pick.

2 Tie a knot in the middle of a 3-inch piece of ribbon. Trim ribbon ends to ¾ inch. Cut notches in ribbon ends with scissors.

3 Glue ribbon knot below monkey's face.

4 Stick pick in frosted cupcake.

Things You'll Need

For Each Cupcake

* ✶ Waterproof tablecloth or plastic trash bags
* ✶ Baked, frosted cupcake
* ✶ ⅝-inch pink-and-white-checked ribbon
* ✶ Plain white paper
* ✶ Wooden cutout shapes: 2 (¾-inch) circles, 1 (1¼-inch) circle, 1 (2-inch) circle
* ✶ Wooden craft pick
* ✶ Paints: white, pink, red
* ✶ Paintbrush
* ✶ Craft glue
* ✶ Regular scissors
* ✶ Black markers with fine and bullet tips
* ✶ Pencil
* ✶ Eraser
* ✶ Ruler

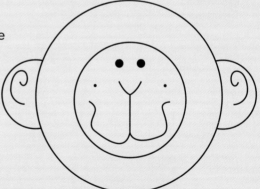

Monkey Cupcake Topper

Bunny Cupcakes

1 Cover work table with tablecloth or plastic bags.

2 Paint the 1¼-inch circle (head) and 1½-inch ovals (ears) white. Paint the ⅜-inch circle (bow-tie knot) and ⅞-inch hearts (bow tie) lemon yellow. Let dry.

Face & Details

1 Use a pencil to trace the bunny's eyes, nose and mouth (below) onto white paper.

2 Turn paper over. Trace over the lines you traced in step 1.

3 Turn the pattern right side up again. Lay it on the white head. Trace over the pattern lines again with a pencil. The lines will now be on the white circle.

4 Dip a dry paintbrush in baby pink paint. Wipe the paint off on a paper towel until almost no more color comes off the brush. Now wipe the brush in a circle on bunny's cheeks, and down centers of ears.

5 Paint nose baby pink.

6 To paint the dots on bow tie, dip the tip of your paintbrush handle into orchid paint. Touch it to the yellow hearts and circle. Let dry.

7 Use the fine tip of the black marker to draw solid lines for eyes and dashed lines for mouth and nose.

8 Use the fine tip of the black marker to draw blanket stitch around edges of head, ears, and pieces for bow tie.

Put It Together

1 Glue the points of the hearts behind the yellow circle to make the bow tie. Glue bow tie to bottom of head.

2 Glue ears to the back side of the head. Glue the head to the wide end of the craft pick.

3 Stick pick in frosted cupcake.

Things You'll Need

For Each Cupcake

* Waterproof tablecloth or plastic trash bags
* Baked, frosted cupcake
* White paper
* Wooden cutout shapes:
  1 (1¼-inch) circle, 1 (⅜-inch) circle, 2 (1½-inch) ovals, 2 (⅞-inch) hearts
* Wooden craft pick
* Paints: white, baby pink, lemon yellow, orchid
* Paintbrush
* Craft glue
* Black fine-tip marker
* Pencil
* Eraser
* Ruler

Bunny Cupcake Topper

Twinkie Centipedes

Things You'll Need
For Each Centipede
* Paper plate
* 1 Twinkie
* 2 miniature marshmallows
* 10 (1-inch) candies for legs (Mike and Ikes, Good and Plenty, Red Hot Tamales, etc.)
* Pretzel sticks
* 2 small round candies for eyes
* Tube icing: pink, green, yellow
* Serving tray

1 Set Twinkie on a paper plate. For legs, stick five 1-inch candies into Twinkie along each long edge.

2 For antennae, break pretzel in half. Stick each piece into a marshmallow.

3 Use icing to hold candy eyes on centipede. Stick pretzel antennae into head behind eyes.

4 Decorate centipede with dots of pink and green icing. Squeeze tiny dots of yellow on each green dot.

5 Arrange centipedes on a serving tray.

Another Idea:

Set bowls of assorted candies and snacks on the table along with tubes and cans of icings and gels. You can offer different shapes of dessert cakes, too, if you want. Invite your guests to create their own awesome bugs. Take each guest's picture with her creepy creation!

Witch's Brew

1 Spoon the sour cream into the large bowl. Sprinkle with pudding mix. Stir until it is mixed well.

2 Gently stir in the pineapple, marshmallows, nuts and cherries.

3 Pour the mixture into the serving bowl. Sprinkle the chocolate chips on top, if you wish. Chill for several hours, or until serving time. Serves 6–8.

Things You'll Need
* 3.4 ounce box of pistachio instant pudding
* 16-ounce container sour cream
* 1 cup crushed pineapple, drained
* 1 cup mini marshmallows
* ½ cup chopped walnuts or pecans
* ½ cup diced cherries, drained
* ¼ cup mini chocolate chips (optional)
* Large bowl
* Spatula
* Measuring cups
* Whisk
* Serving dish

Pumpkin Pudding Treats

Painting

1 Cover worktable with tablecloth or plastic bags. Turn pudding cup upside-down on work table.

2 Cut out pattern for pumpkin chest leaf (page 190). Use a pencil to trace two leaves onto green craft foam.

3 Mix a little yellow and bright green paint on paper plate. Dip sponge in paint. Dab it lightly over leaves. You do not have to cover the foam completely.

4 Let paint dry for 1 hour. Cut out leaves along pencil lines.

5 Use fine-tip marker to draw outline of squiggles and dots around edges.

6 Mix a little orange and yellow paint on paper plate. Dip clean sponge in paint. Dab it over outside of pudding cup. Let dry.

7 Press a small piece of double-stick tape onto the paper plate. Stick wooden plug on tape. Paint plug red for nose. Let dry.

Put It Together

1 Glue leaves on top of pudding cup.

2 Wrap the chenille stem around a pencil to make a coil. Slide coil off. Glue one end in center of leaves.

3 Glue eyes and nose to side of cup. Draw a squiggly smile and eyebrows with black paint. Paint white highlight on nose. Let dry.

4 Wrap purple ribbon around base of cup. Tie ends in a bow on the front.

Things You'll Need
For Each Treat

* Waterproof tablecloth or plastic trash bags
* Pudding snack cup: vanilla, butterscotch or orange (use a kind that doesn't need to be refrigerated)
* Green craft foam
* 4-inch piece green pipe cleaner
* ½-inch wooden plug
* 2 (6mm) wiggly eyes
* ¼-inch-wide purple satin ribbon
* Paint for plastic*: orange, yellow, bright green, red
* Paint for paper*: white, black
* Small paintbrush
* 1-inch pieces cut from a clean kitchen sponge
* Black permanent fine-tip marker
* Double-stick tape
* Paper plate
* Container of water
* Paper towels
* Craft glue
* Toothpick
* Scissors
* Pencil
* Ruler

*Paints for plastic and paper from Plaid Enterprises were used for these projects.

Ho Ho Ponies

1 Work on a piece of waxed paper or a paper plate to put your pony together. Cut four 1½-inch pieces from the Tootsie Rolls. Stick a toothpick in one end of each leg. Stick the other ends into the Ho Ho (body) for legs.

2 Cut a 1-inch piece of Tootsie Roll for the neck. Break a toothpick in half. Stick one piece in both ends of the neck. Press one end into the top of the Ho Ho.

3 Use the knife to cut small slits into a 1-inch slice of taffy. Press it onto the side of the neck for the mane.

4 Cut small snips in the rounded top part of the jelly slice to form ears. Press onto the top of the toothpick on the neck for the head.

5 Cut a 2-inch slice of taffy. Cut 1-inch slits in it. Roll it into a tube shape. Break a toothpick in half. Press half into the tail area of the body. Press the taffy onto the other end to form the tail.

Things You'll Need
For each pony:
* Waterproof tablecloth or plastic trash bags
* One Ho Ho cake roll
* Tootsie Rolls
* Red taffy candy
* Red jelly "fruit slice" candy
* Toothpicks
* Clean small scissors
* Waxed paper or paper plate
* Knife

Santa Face Cake

Let's Begin

1 Ask an adult to preheat the oven to the temperature listed for your pan size on the box of cake mix.

2 Grease and flour the cake pan.

3 Mix the cake batter following the instructions on the box of cake mix.

4 Pour the batter in the pan. Bake following the instructions on the box. *Note: If you have extra batter, use it to make cupcakes.*

5 Ask an adult to take the hot cake out of the oven and tip it out of the pan, onto a cooling rack. Let cake cool completely.

6 Place paper doily on plate. Turn cake upside down onto doily. Point of cake will be tip of Santa's hat.

Frost the Cake

1 For beard, use knife to spread white frosting on the bottom, rounded half of the cake. (Look at the photo.)

2 For face, place a small amount of white frosting in a small bowl. To make it pink, add a very small drop of red food coloring. Mix well. Spread the pink frosting in a 1½-inch strip above the white frosting.

3 To make red frosting for the hat, add more red food coloring to the remaining pink and white frosting. Mix well. Spread the red frosting on the pointed top of cake.

Decorate the Cake

1 For the nose, stack three pink Sweet Tarts at the top center of the beard. Add a little frosting between the tarts to hold them together.

2 For the beard, press on marshmallows to cover all of the white frosting.

3 For the eyes, press blue M&M's onto face.

4 For the hat brim, press white drop candies along the bottom edge of the red frosting.

5 Press a peppermint candy onto the tip of the hat.

Things You'll Need

* Cake mix *plus* ingredients to make it
* Tub of white frosting
* Red food coloring
* White miniature marshmallows
* 3 pink Sweet Tarts
* 2 blue M&M's
* 1 peppermint candy
* White chocolate drops with red, white and green sprinkles
* Heart-shaped cake pan
* Paper doily (as large as cake)
* Mixer
* Mixing bowl
* Spoon
* Rubber scraper
* Cooling rack
* Small bowl
* Knife

Food Fun—Beverages

Cool off from your party games with one of these refreshing and fun-to-make beverages!

Strawberry Sipper

1 Put frozen strawberries in blender first, then add orange juice. Add crushed ice. Put the cover on the blender and blend for 1 minute or until everything is mixed well.

2 If the drink is too thick, add a little more orange juice. Pour into two tall glasses. Add fresh strawberries and straws.

Note: Pineapple juice can be used if you like a sweeter taste. Frozen sweetened raspberries can be used instead of frozen strawberries.

Things You'll Need
* 10-ounce package of sweetened frozen strawberries
* 2 cups crushed ice
* ¾ cup orange juice
* Fresh strawberries
* Blender
* Long wooden spoon
* 2 tall glasses
* 2 straws

Super Cool Drinks

1 Mix drink mix powder with 1 cup sugar and 2 quarts water in pitcher. Stir until sugar and drink mix are dissolved.

2 Fill ice-cube trays half-full with mixture. Freeze. Add frozen cubes of different colors to cold drinks.

Frozen Pops: Mix your favorite flavor of powdered drink mix. Pour it into ice cube trays. Cover with plastic wrap. Put in freezer for 30 minutes. Take tray out of freezer, but leave plastic on. Gently poke a toothpick through plastic wrap into each section. Put back in freezer until frozen. Remove from freezer and take off plastic wrap.

Things You'll Need
* Different flavors of powdered drink mixes
* Sugar
* 2-quart pitcher
* Mixing spoon
* Ice cube trays
* Toothpicks
* Plastic wrap

Faux Champagne

 Mix a few drops of food coloring into the soda to give it a nice pink color.

 Pour your "champagne" into chilled champagne glasses.

 Cut a slit in each strawberry. Slide a berry onto the rim of each glass.

Things You'll Need
* Sparking apple cider, ginger ale or lemon-lime soda
* Red food coloring
* Whole, washed strawberries
* Paring knife

Sparkling Water with Frozen Strawberries

The day before your party:

 Cover a plate with plastic wrap.

 Remove stems from strawberries. Stand strawberries up on plate. Set plate of berries in freezer.

When ready to serve:

 Remove frozen berries from freezer.

 Fill glasses with sparkling water or club soda. Drop in one or two frozen strawberries.

 Hook a lime slice over the edge of each glass. Add a straw.

ings You'll Need
* Whole, fresh strawberries
* Sparkling water or club soda
* Slices of lime
* Tall, clear drinking glasses
* Straws
* Plate
* Plastic wrap

Marbleized Milk

 Squeeze syrup in milk.

 Just barely mix flavored syrup through milk. Do not over mix so swirls will show.

 Insert a straw and serve to your guests.

Things You'll Need
* Milk
* Flavored syrups
* Plastic straws

Icy-Cold Fruit Juice

Serve your favorite fruit juice with plenty of crushed ice and call it "sea slush." If you use ice cubes, call them "icebergs."

Pop Star Punch

Things You'll Need
* Fruit juice
* Ginger ale
* Maraschino cherries

1 Pour fruit juice into ice-cube trays. Fill about two-thirds full. Place a cherry in each section. Freeze.

2 When ready to serve, place several ice cubes in a glass. Pour ginger ale over ice cubes.

Iced Fruit Tea

Brew a big batch of your favorite herbal fruit tea. Sweeten to taste. Add thin slices of lemon to the pitcher. Chill the tea in the refrigerator.

Serve in tall glasses with Fancy Flower Drinking Straws (page 103).

Root Beer Floats

Place several scoops of vanilla ice cream in a frosty glass mug. Fill with cold root beer. Add a colored straw or long-handled spoon for scooping the foam.

Things You'll Need
* Ginger ale or lemon-lime soda
* Red food coloring
* Whole cleaned strawberries

Pink Champagne

1 Serve chilled in champagne glasses.

2 Mix food coloring into soda prior to serving.

3 Top with a strawberry set on glass rim.

Fruit Punch

Mix equal parts water and lemon lime soda with unsweetened drink mix. Pour into clear glasses and serve with umbrella straws.

Drop in a gummy ring "life preserver" for extra fun.

Things You'll Need
* 1 envelope unsweetened powdered drink mix
* Water
* Lemon-lime soda
* Peach gummy rings

Ice-Cream Shake

The fun is having your guests choose which combination of flavors they want to mix!

Let's Begin

1 Place ice cubes and 1 cup of milk in blender. Blend until there are small chips of ice.

2 Drop scoops of ice cream in blender. Add syrup and fruit to taste. Blend until creamy. Add small amount of milk if needed.

3 Pour shake into glasses. Put whipped cream on top and place a piece of fruit in the whipped cream. Insert a straw.

Things You'll Need
* Ice cream: vanilla, chocolate, cherry
* Syrups: chocolate, strawberry, caramel, butterscotch
* Fruit: strawberries, bananas, pineapple, cherries
* Milk
* Whipped cream
* Ice
* Ice cream scoop
* Straws
* Blender

Purple Milkshakes

Mix purple Kool-Aid with vanilla ice cream and milk in a blender.

Pattern Pages

Concert Ticket **from page 12**

admission
music party

date:
time:
location:

Fairy Dust Invitation

from page 41

Fairy Dance
Held in Celebration of:

Date:
Time:
Location:

Please bring a 6" x 8"
Memory Book with a white
cover to the party.

RSVP:

Slumber Fun Sleepover **from page 23**

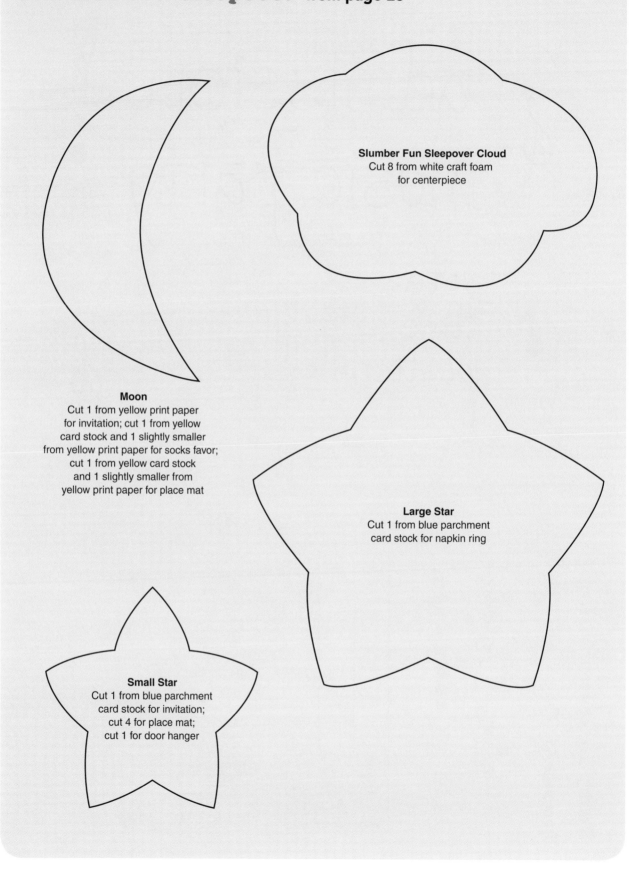

Slumber Fun Sleepover Cloud
Cut 8 from white craft foam
for centerpiece

Moon
Cut 1 from yellow print paper
for invitation; cut 1 from yellow
card stock and 1 slightly smaller
from yellow print paper for socks favor;
cut 1 from yellow card stock
and 1 slightly smaller from
yellow print paper for place mat

Large Star
Cut 1 from blue parchment
card stock for napkin ring

Small Star
Cut 1 from blue parchment
card stock for invitation;
cut 4 for place mat;
cut 1 for door hanger

Girlfriend Charm Bracelets **from page 35**

Fairy Dance Memory Book from page 44

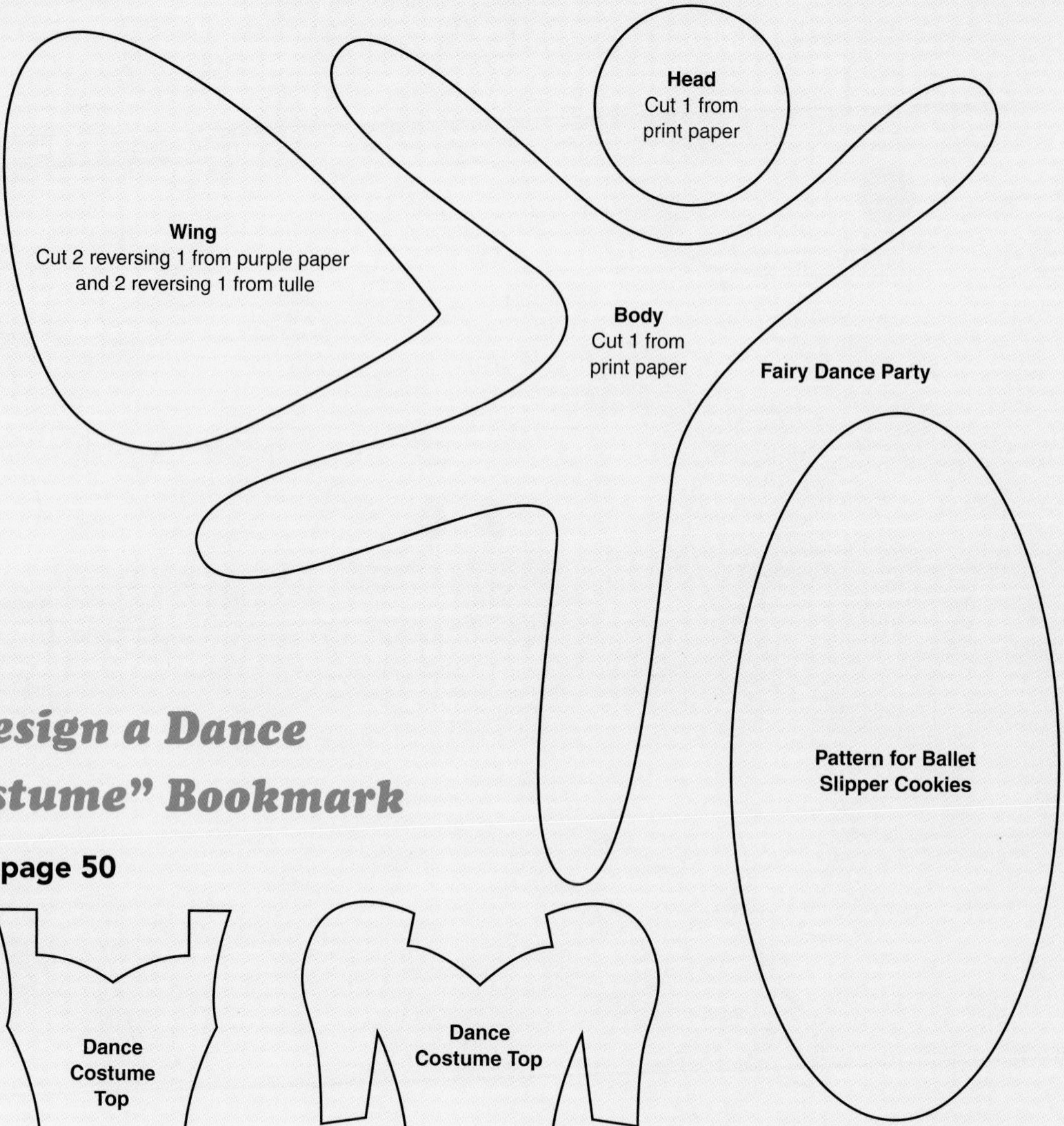

Head
Cut 1 from
print paper

Wing
Cut 2 reversing 1 from purple paper
and 2 reversing 1 from tulle

Body
Cut 1 from
print paper

Fairy Dance Party

"Design a Dance Costume" Bookmark

from page 50

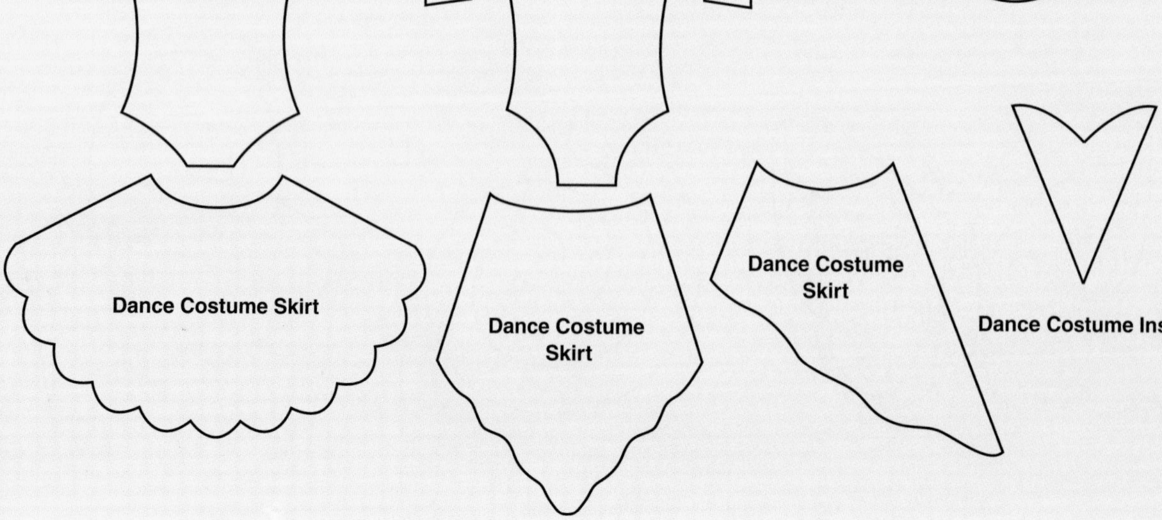

Pattern for Ballet Slipper Cookies

Dance
Costume
Top

Dance
Costume Top

Dance Costume Skirt

Dance Costume
Skirt

Dance Costume
Skirt

Dance Costume Inset

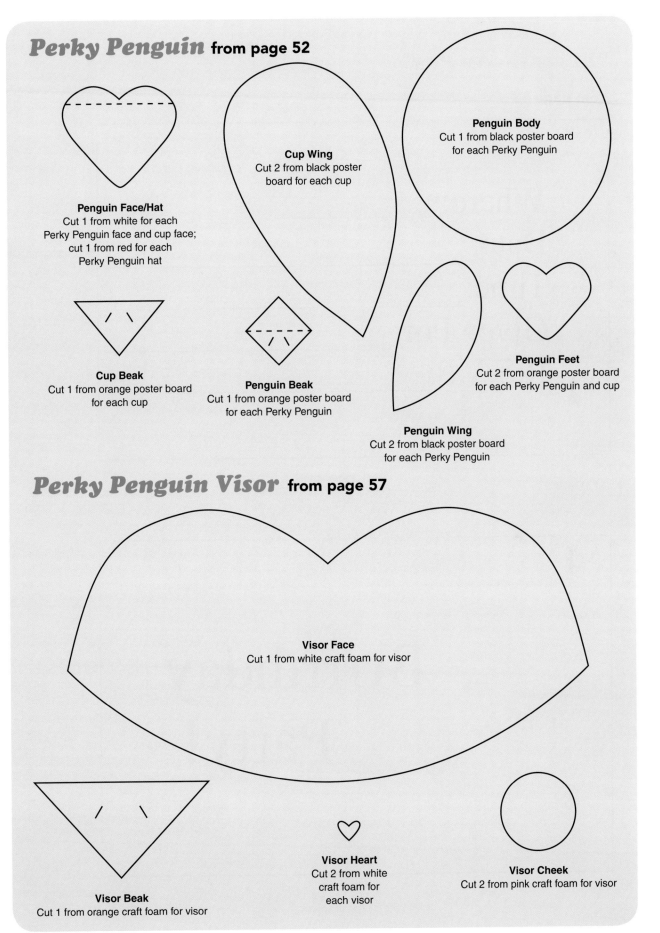

Perky Penguin from page 52

Penguin Face/Hat
Cut 1 from white for each
Perky Penguin face and cup face;
cut 1 from red for each
Perky Penguin hat

Cup Wing
Cut 2 from black poster
board for each cup

Penguin Body
Cut 1 from black poster board
for each Perky Penguin

Cup Beak
Cut 1 from orange poster board
for each cup

Penguin Beak
Cut 1 from orange poster board
for each Perky Penguin

Penguin Feet
Cut 2 from orange poster board
for each Perky Penguin and cup

Penguin Wing
Cut 2 from black poster board
for each Perky Penguin

Perky Penguin Visor from page 57

Visor Face
Cut 1 from white craft foam for visor

Visor Beak
Cut 1 from orange craft foam for visor

Visor Heart
Cut 2 from white
craft foam for
each visor

Visor Cheek
Cut 2 from pink craft foam for visor

"Brrrrthday Party! Invitation

from page 53

Where: ____________________

Date: ____________________

Time: ____________________

Given For: ____________________

R.S.V.P: ____________________

← Cutting line

Party Information
Trace or photocopy 1 for each invitation;
dashed line is edge of snowflake frame

Brrrrthday
Party!

← Cutting line

Trace or photocopy 1 for each invitation;
dashed line is edge of snowflake frame

Artist's Palette from page 97

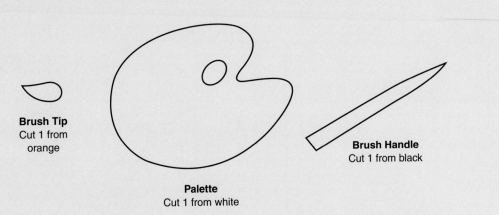

Brush Tip
Cut 1 from
orange

Palette
Cut 1 from white

Brush Handle
Cut 1 from black

Flip Flops from pages 76, 163

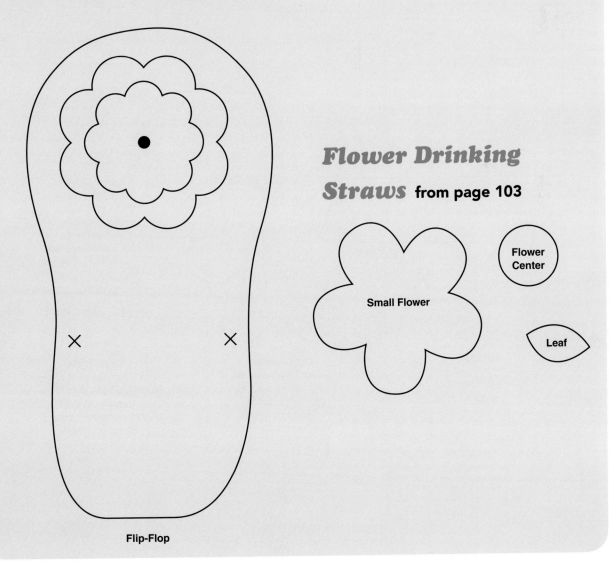

Flip-Flop

Flower Drinking Straws from page 103

Small Flower

Flower Center

Leaf

Scrapbooking Party from page 78

Pocket
Cut 1 per each guest
from assorted bright
colors for each pair
scrapbook pages

Fold

Large Flower
Cut 1 from orange
for Invitation
and 1 from bright
color for Goody Bag.
Cut 7 assorted for each
pair Scrapbook Pages.

Large Circle
Cut 1 from yellow
for each Invitation
and Goody Bag.
Cut 7 yellow for
each pair Scrapbook
Pages.

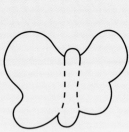

Butterfly
Cut 1 from pink for
each pair scrapbook
pages.

Small Flower
Cut 1 from blue for
invitation; cut 1 for
each Table Decoration,
Napkin and Cup.
Cut 7 assorted for each
pair Scrapbook Pages.

Small Circle
Cut 1 from yellow for each
Inviation, Table Decoration,
Napkin and Cup.
Cut 7 yellow for each pair
Scrapbook Pages.

Pony Pony Lights from page 85

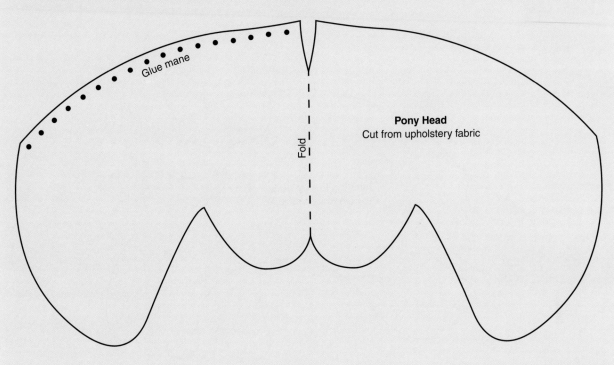

Glue mane

Fold

Pony Head
Cut from upholstery fabric

Pony Head from page 84

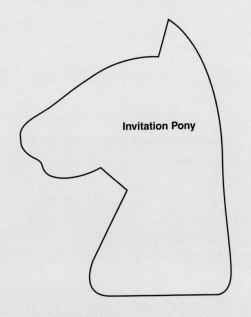

Invitation Pony

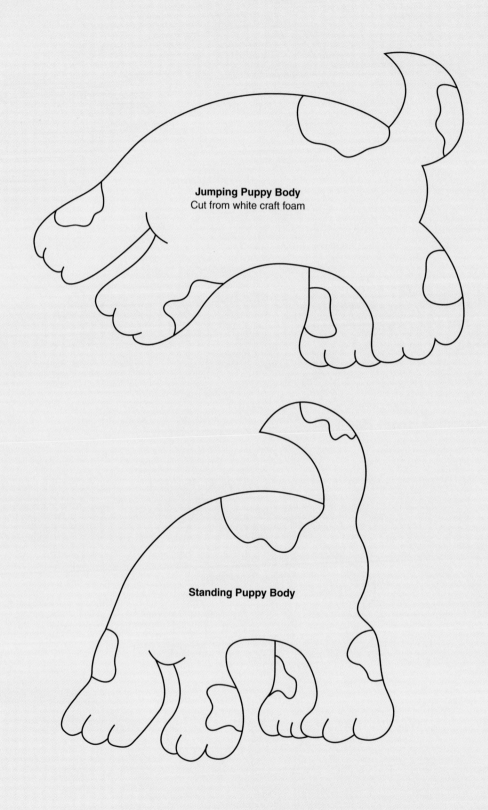

Jumping Puppy Body
Cut from white craft foam

Standing Puppy Body

Kitty & Puppy Party

from page 91

Standing Kitty Body

Jumping Kitty Body
Cut from pink craft foam

Puppy Head
Cut from white
craft foam

Small Tail
Cut 1 from
blue parchment
for each invitation

Kitty Head
Cut from pink
craft foam

"Toadally Yours" Invitation **from page 113**

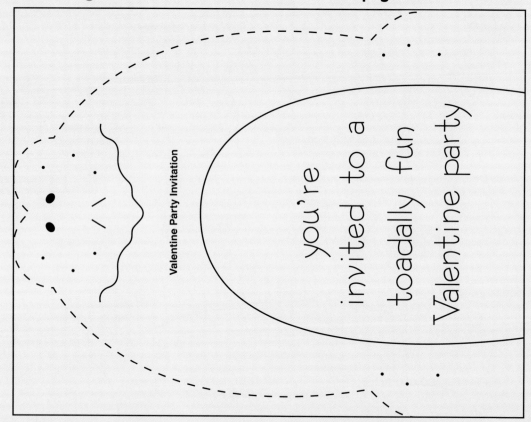

Valentine Party Invitation

you're invited to a toadally fun Valentine party

Kitty Candy Bag

from page 116

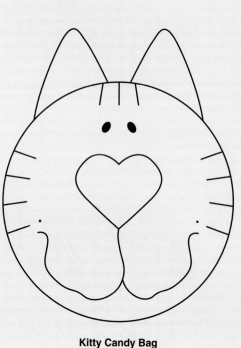

Kitty Candy Bag

Drop the Lovebugs in the Jar

from page 117

hugs inside

Heart for Lovebugs in a Jar

Valentine Puppy Pouch from page 114

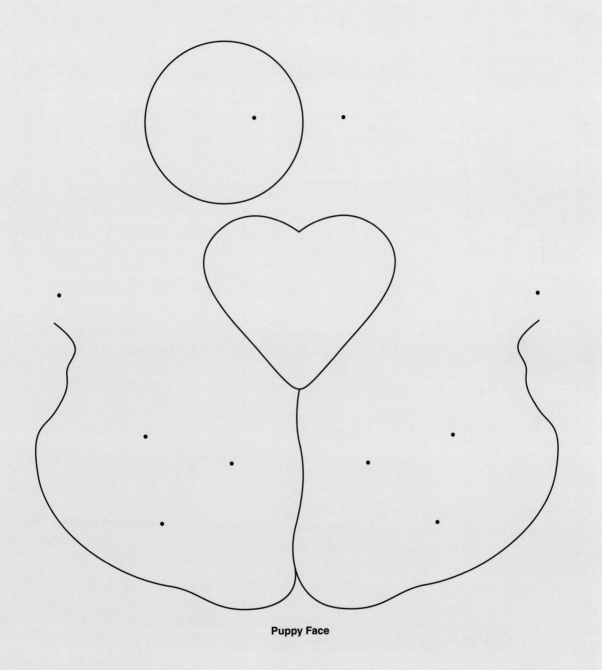

Puppy Face

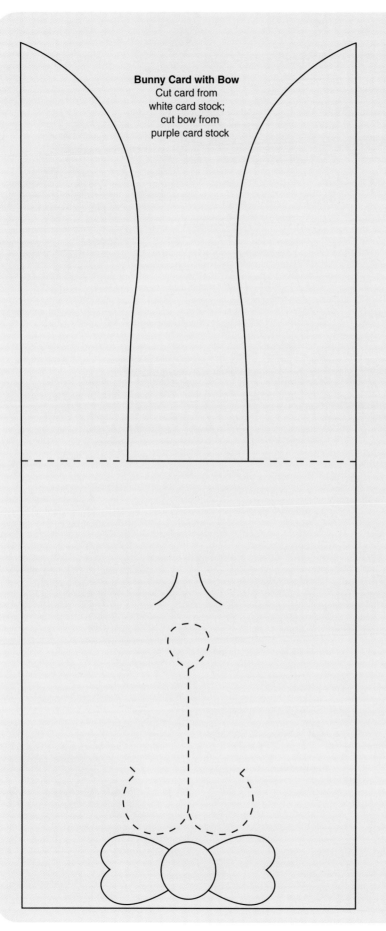

Bunny Card with Bow
Cut card from
white card stock;
cut bow from
purple card stock

Bunny Invitation

from page 118

Bunny Bag and Bunny Shaker from pages 119, 122

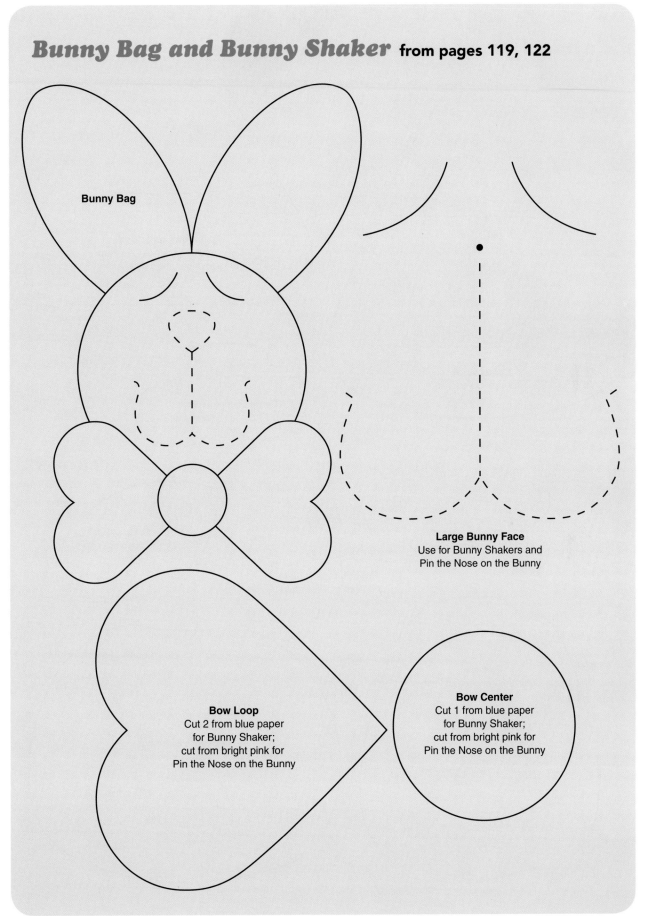

Bunny Bag

Large Bunny Face
Use for Bunny Shakers and
Pin the Nose on the Bunny

Bow Loop
Cut 2 from blue paper
for Bunny Shaker;
cut from bright pink for
Pin the Nose on the Bunny

Bow Center
Cut 1 from blue paper
for Bunny Shaker;
cut from bright pink for
Pin the Nose on the Bunny

Candy-Corny Invitation **from page 123**

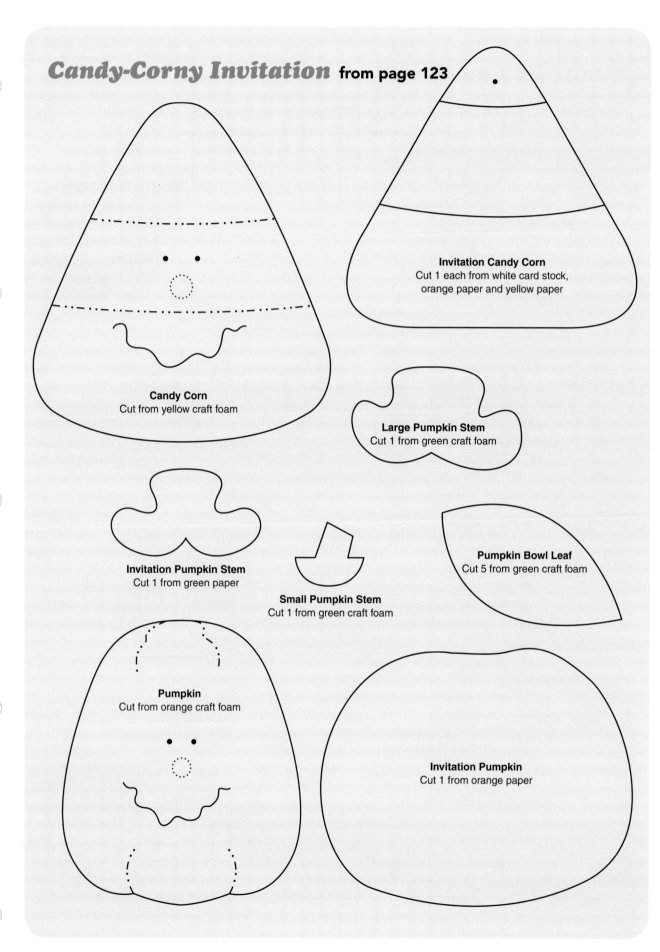

Invitation Candy Corn
Cut 1 each from white card stock,
orange paper and yellow paper

Candy Corn
Cut from yellow craft foam

Large Pumpkin Stem
Cut 1 from green craft foam

Invitation Pumpkin Stem
Cut 1 from green paper

Small Pumpkin Stem
Cut 1 from green craft foam

Pumpkin Bowl Leaf
Cut 5 from green craft foam

Pumpkin
Cut from orange craft foam

Invitation Pumpkin
Cut 1 from orange paper

Fall Bead Necklaces

from page 128

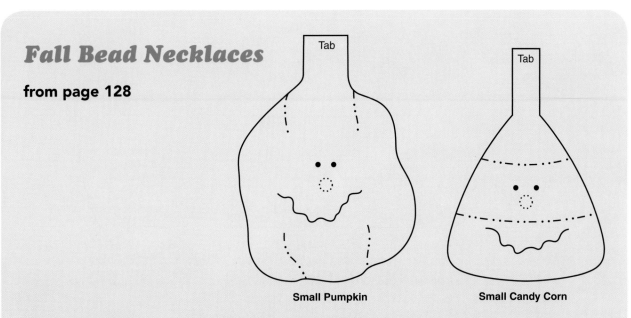

Small Pumpkin

Small Candy Corn

Secret Santa Party Invitation from page 130

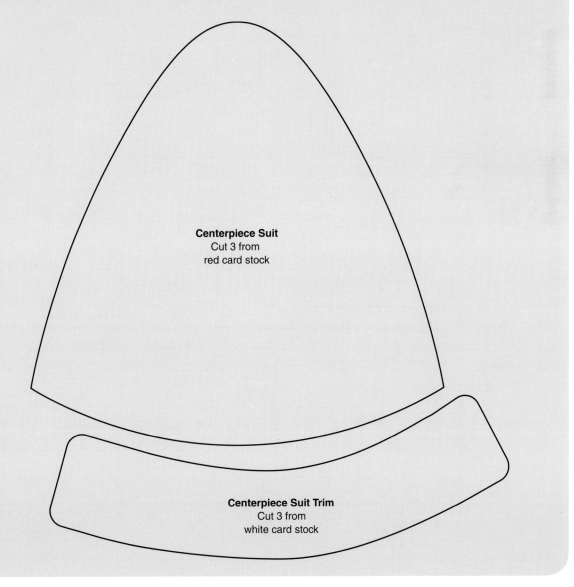

Centerpiece Suit
Cut 3 from
red card stock

Centerpiece Suit Trim
Cut 3 from
white card stock

Secret Santa Party Invitation from page 130

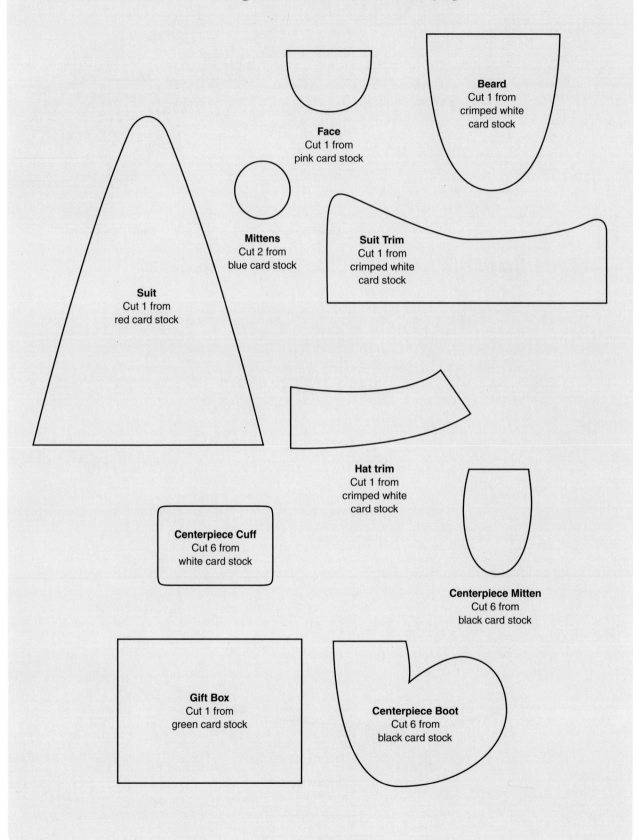

Face
Cut 1 from
pink card stock

Beard
Cut 1 from
crimped white
card stock

Mittens
Cut 2 from
blue card stock

Suit Trim
Cut 1 from
crimped white
card stock

Suit
Cut 1 from
red card stock

Hat trim
Cut 1 from
crimped white
card stock

Centerpiece Cuff
Cut 6 from
white card stock

Centerpiece Mitten
Cut 6 from
black card stock

Gift Box
Cut 1 from
green card stock

Centerpiece Boot
Cut 6 from
black card stock